UNCOVER THE MISSING

PEACE

Dissolve Resentment

Avoid Anger

UNCOVER THE MISSING PEACE
Dissolve Resentment Avoid Anger

Copyright © 2015 by Dr. Lewis C. Baskins

ISBN-13: 978-1517445492

ISBN-10: 1517445493

DEDICATION

This book is dedicated to (the memory of) S.B. Fuller, the man that, more than any other human, assisted me onto the path of Truth. To Fuller and all the "Fuller-ites" on both sides of the veil, I am grateful that Mr. Fuller encouraged each Fuller-ite to make the following affirmative prayer a part of his/her daily life:

The Soul's Sincere Desire
- Glenn Clark (1925)

Our Heavenly Father, we know that thy Love is as Infinite as the
sky is infinite,
and thy ways of manifesting that love are as unaccountable
as the stars of the heavens.

Thy Power is greater than man's horizon
and thy ways of manifesting that Power
are more numerous than the sands of the sea.

As thou keepest the stars in their courses,
so shalt Thou guide our steps in perfect harmony,
without clash or discord of any kind, if we keep our trust in Thee.
For we know Thou wilt keep him in perfect peace whose mind is
stayed on Thee,
because he trusteth in Thee. We know that, if we acknowledge
Thee in all our ways,
Thou will direct our paths. For Thou art the God of Love,
Giver of every good and perfect gift, and there is none beside
Thee.
Thou are omnipotent, omniscient, and omnipresent,
in all, through all, and over all, the only God.
And Thine is the Kingdom, and the Power and the Glory, forever,
Amen.

ACKNOWLEDGEMENTS

My appreciation and gratitude is hereby expressed to the many individuals who have been instruments through whom inspiration and physical activity have assisted me in my personal growth and the writing of this book.

Paramount in my gratitude and acknowledgement is for the Universal Divine Spirit which is the Source and substance of all things visible and invisible, which include the idea for this book.

Having recently retired from being a dentist for over half a century, my thanks to the thousands of dental patients I have been fortunate to serve, many of whom have become lifelong friends, and many have transitioned into the next parenthesis (-) of eternity.

Thanks to the Infinite Invisible for expressing Itself as Betty Muhammad whom I love and present together in schools, churches, on cable television, radio and the internet. She is a center of Light that has benefited me and many others in the human family. Thanks, Betty.

To B'Lov Smith, thank you for your friendship and encouragement and support over the years.

My sister, Louvenia Baskins Williams offered invaluable support in multiple ways, including design of the original book cover to express a central theme of this book, that peace is uncovered in the Now silence, not past, present nor future through human thought.

Burma James' help in editing and transcribing manuscript, and the lively conversations is highly appreciated.

My beautiful and gifted daughter, Holly Baskins Spears, has always been a source of joy and inspiration beyond what words can describe.

Thanks to my son, Brian Scott Baskins, for writing his book, *Oneness: Principles of World Peace* (Book 1 in The Message of Global Unity Series), and guiding me through the maze of bringing this book to fruition.

Dora Clark, thank you for your input toward this book-writing project. Your friendship and support is greatly appreciated.

To all of my chess-playing friends, you have served well in teaching me awareness, patience and other virtues acquired.

My eternal gratitude for the unwavering support and encouragement received from my two other sons, Duane Mercer Baskins and Kevin Eric Baskins. I appreciate you.

My supreme thanks is to you, the reader. May we all continue to unfold on the path of Truth and enlightenment that this parenthesis of human experience will, by a ripple effect, be an influence for generations yet to come to live in fulfillment and peace.

FOREWORD

"Ignorance is the root of misfortune" is a statement often made by my mentor, S.B. Fuller. The true enemy of man is ignorance of his True Identity.

Be clear, the word "ignorance" simply means "a lack of understanding." It is not related to schooling or formal education. An individual can be an educated "sophisticated ignoramus," and still be unaware of one's True Self.

Throughout this first book, I am aware of the repetition of certain ideas expressed. This is done to remind and emphasize to the reader that idea; that it may find a home in the consciousness of the reader.

God made within man His image and likeness. However, the strings of attachment to culture, tradition, habits and emotions keep humanity enslaved in the fog of ignorance; this fog is the obstruction that covers peace, harmony and joy.

Humanity is on an eternal search for fulfillment and peace. His search is in the external realm, whereas peace and fulfillment can only be found within his own being. "The kingdom of God is within you." (Luke 17:21)

"Within you" does not mean inside of your body. The liver, heart and other vital organs are inside your body, but "within" means the very essence of one's being; that of which one is constituted.

A table made of oak wood is not separate and apart from the oak. Oakwood is *within* the table, for they are one and same.

"I and my father are one." Spirit is the father of all of us, because this is an all-spiritual universe.

The illusion that leads to conflict between individuals and/or nations is caused by a faulty belief system of duality, separation. Man's eternal search for fulfillment and the missing peace shall be realized only through the awakening to the "I" that already exists within.

The personal identity of race, religion, nationality and other illusions that appear to separate, will no longer exist.

The reader of this book is encouraged not to judge the message offered through the screen of what you think you already know. That is not to suggest that you accept what is being offered, simply remain open. If the message finds a home in your consciousness or not remains to be seen. Do not judge from what you think you already know, thereby leaving open an opportunity for growth.

There are many answers to human problems…but *only one* solution: Awakening to one's True Spiritual Identity, then living by grace. Only something that already exists can be uncovered; peace already exists within you NOW!

Being raised as a child in a Baptist Christian church is the thread that underlies using biblical quotations throughout this book. The quotations and references are in the context of my understanding the Bible as a book of wisdom to lift anyone into a higher state of consciousness of the Spiritual Oneness of the universe.

The front cover of this book illustrates the apparent deadness of the human state of consciousness; which covers peace, harmony and joy in the human experience of Life.

CONTENTS

THE SEARCH BEGINS 10

THE PATH TO PEACE 11

MY WORD, MY WORLD..16

ATTAINING THE PEACE OF *I* 18

DROP YOUR NET OF GETTING, TO LETTING 19

GIFTS AND TALENTS..22

ANY OF MANY 24

COMMUNICATE, COOPERATE, COORDINATE = SUCCESS 25

NON-REACTION, BE A BEHOLDER 28

AMAZING GRACE...31

THE MIRACLE OF PEACE..33

SELF-SACRIFICE 34

FLOWERS OF LIFE 35

THE SECRET PEACE PLACE 38

SPIRITUALITY, THE GOLDEN SUBSTANCE OF PEACE 45

IT IS AS IT IS 50

THE PATH TO PEACE 54

ONENESS 58

THE WOMB OF SILENCE 66

DEMONSTRATE LEADERSHIP IN ACTION 68

GROUP DYNAMICS 69

YOUR WORD BECOMES YOUR WORLD 72

SOWING AND REAPING 73

INNER SELF TALK 75

"AS A MAN THINKETH IN HIS HEART, SO IS HE".............................76

NO DIRTY WATER 78

I HAVE...80

THOUGHTS TO PONDER 81

THE TOMB OF IGNORANCE 81

PRODIGAL SON 82

OMNIPRESENT (ALWAYS NOW), AND OMNIPRESENCE (ALWAYS
HERE) 83

UNVEIL THE LIGHT OF TRUTH BY AWAKENING TO TRUTH
IDENTITY 85

DIS-EASE BRINGS ABOUT DISEASE 86

CONVERSATIONS FOR TRANSFORMATION....................................87

AVOID STRESS, SILENCE THE MIND 88

THE PRISON OF FEAR, IGNORANCE...93

IMPERSONALIZATION..93

POWER OF SILENCE..96

THE HYPNOSIS OF HUMANHOOD: BELIEFS.................................97

AGAIN, SEX, THAT HUSH-HUSH TOPIC..107

AWARENESS...109

GRAINS OF TRUTH (WILL GROW WHEN RECEIVED IN FERTILE GROUND/CONSCIOUSNESS) 111
SUPPLY 112
VICTOR OR VICTIM 113
"I" IS A PRINTOUT OF THE DIVINE 115
LITTLE THINGS MEAN A LOT 117
PEACE, BE STILL 120
ANGER AVOIDANCE 121
THE UNCHANGING REQUISITES OF LEADERSHIP – S. B. FULLER ... 124
EDUCATION PROCESS – S. B. FULLER 124
BEYOND THE HORIZON 125
THE PURSUIT OF HAPPINESS 127
ILLUSIONS 128
SELF RELIANCE 131

THE SEARCH BEGINS

Each of us has a spark of Divinity within and each must learn to fan that spark individually for one's self and the uplifting of mankind. That spark is our source of existence. No human knows how to make a sperm nor an egg. That which sprang forth from the invisible as sperm remains within, bringing us through infancy, childhood, adolescence to physical maturity. That spark of energy we call *"I." "I* will never leave you nor forsake you." *I* will be with you until the end of the world as humans know it. *I* create the attraction between male/female that brings forth the sperm cells to fertilize the egg. *"I"* is within the individual. This substance, this power will never leave you because it *is* you and you are it. "I and my Father are one" (John 10:30). "Call no man on earth your father." (Matthew 23:9) There is no separation except as an illusion or hypnosis. The day or moment you accept a belief of duality you die to the knowledge and understanding of oneness of the universe. (Gen. 2:17) One word made manifest as many units of expression.

Man in his True Identity is an individualization of that we call God. When we speak of "man," that includes male and female of the human family and everything else that has form or that is *man*-ifested (minerals, plants and animals). One substance, Spirit, that is forever expressing *as* you, cannot leave nor forsake you. This is a Spiritual Universe. Therefore the Source of my beginning is yet with me, *as* me, eternally. To seek guidance from the Source is to perpetuate the human sense of separation from God, whereas there never has been a separation in Reality. The individual must awaken from the dream, the hypnosis of the world. Be in the world, but not of the world's belief system. "Ye shall know the truth and the truth shall make you free."

All life form feels or calls itself by the identifying code *"I."* The ant, elephant, tiger, etc. feels *"I* am in danger." Certainly not using human language, but as self-identification. Do not we humans feel and say *"I"* throughout our life; *I* am on the phone, angry, hungry, sleepy or whatever.

The bit of life that shows forth as sperm and/or egg from the invisible world of spirit must identify itself as *"I"* also. This *I* shows forth as the unborn embryo, the infant, child, teenager and adult human. All stages of human physical and mental development come from within the individual. *"I* will never leave you nor forsake you." Every visible thing is an expression of this invisible *I.* The individual human comes *through* our parents. We certainly did not come *from* them. "Call no man your father on earth." Again, no man or woman on earth knows how to make sperm or egg, which appears as each individual's beginning.

The source and substance that is expressing as you and me is one of peace, harmony and joy. To seek guidance from some outside authority is to maintain a sense of separation from the *oneness*, which is God. There are always those outer "authority" figures, who are equally unawakened, ready to offer their opinions. We must go within for directions for peace. When a wise illumined individual points to the moon, all that the ignorant see is the finger pointing. No one is responsible for the awakening of another to illumination of truth. Anyone, who is open and receptive, can receive understanding and know peace. The individual search for peace is continuous for humans. It is only through an awakening to the Truth that we are spiritual beings and gaining an awareness, knowledge and understanding of our oneness with the source of all creation, that peace and fulfillment are realized and experienced. Awaken to your True Identity now.

THE PATH TO PEACE

Everyone is on the path to some degree. When we think of pathways there arises in the mind the concept of space and time. Both time and space are illusions perpetuated by the universal belief systems. In reality, there is only *here* and *now*. The tree only knows NOW! Let us use an image of a figure in the form of a cross. We recognize this to be a religious symbol for many people, but it can also serve an individual in another manner: to remind the person that he has the privilege of *choice*.

The horizontal and vertical lines intersect at a point of *choice*. Let's say the horizontal line represents time (past, present, future). Most human minds use the present moment to play old

11

tapes in memory of the past, or be anxious in anticipation of the future. There are many sleepless nights caused by focus on the past or future. To focus on past or future is to obscure the *Now*.

You can choose to neutralize this preoccupation with the past and future by practicing being aware of the *Now* moment – PMA (Present Moment Awareness). Being present in the here and now removes time, the linear aspect of the cross.

The vertical aspect of the cross represents here and now, being in the present moment. Where the vertical and horizontal images of the cross intersect represents a point of choice, becoming aware of where you are dwelling – in a sense of time or meditating in the here and now, where peace is dis-covered, uncovered! Get out of the mind; peace, be still.

God, peace, is to be experienced only in the Now. God is always omnipresence, Here, and omnipresent, Now! Human beings have at least five major appetites that can cause addictions to seem to move one out of here and now:

1. Stomach appetite (food overeating, smoking, alcohol, drugs, etc.)
2. Sex appetite (always seeking stimulation of sex)
3. Greed appetite (gambling, stealing, cheating, etc.)
4. Religion (becoming a religious zealot, fanatic)
5. Power (the desire to control, or influence others)

These, and more, tempt humans to ignore the Here and Now. Lest we forget, the root word "ignore" gives us the word *ignorant,* which simply means a lack of understanding of the principles of Here and Now. As one realizes omnipresence (omni plus present), one begins to live by the activity of Grace and not worry about the past or future and be at peace. Yesterday ended last night! Destroy those old tapes of the past by becoming aware of the present moment of Now. The momentum of habit of the mind entertaining thoughts must be recognized and neutralized by practicing awareness of Now.

"The Son (Sun) of man cometh when you think not." This does not mean coming by surprise, but when you are not thinking.

To be released from the control of impressions from the past, you must shatter the myth of linearity of time – past, present, future – and awaken to the eternality of Now. Ask yourself what is it that is being *aware* of your finger or your breathing? It certainly is not thought. It is consciousness, *"I,"* that is being aware. As one rises in consciousness the greater the peace of mind from thoughts of the past or future. Live in the *Now* moment of *Is*. Abide in that word and let that word abide in your consciousness. The word *IS* equals the word *NOW*.

If an individual is constantly worrying about what is going to happen in the future, one will miss living for the joy of the present moment of *Now*. And the past is kept alive only in memory. Memory is a wonderful gift by the Creator, but as with the gifts of water, fire and electricity, each will destroy an individual when misused or abused. The mind in its most effective usage ought to be a clear transparency for the Inner Light to communicate with the individual. As an example; the sunlight does not come *from* the clear transparent windowpane, but it comes *through* the transparency of the glass. If there is mud or some other obstruction on the pane, the light will not come through. In a similar sense if there is mud on the mind, in the form of thoughts, that Inner Light cannot come through and that still, quiet voice from within will not be received. *"Speak Lord, thou servant heareth."*

The momentum of habit of the mind entertaining thoughts must be recognized and neutralized by practicing awareness of *Now*. Do the following exercise:

Without moving or looking at it, how do you know that your left hand exists? The moment that you read or heard the question, you became *aware* of your left hand! You were not *thinking* of your hand, but *aware* of your left hand.

Awareness causes thoughts to cease, stand still. You can practice being aware of each of your ten fingers in sequence or of your breathing. One cannot be *aware* and entertain thoughts at the same time.

Because of the habit of your mind entertaining thoughts, they will still come as you practice awareness. Do not resist them but let them drift on by as a cloud drifting by in the sky and get back to being aware of your fingers or whatever. This practice of awareness alerts the individual of how to be in the *Now* Moment and not to live in the linear fashion of past and future. Remember the vertical aspect of the Cross analogy? Living in the *Now* moment assures one of experiencing peace.

This silence of thoughts is the gateway to meditation or true prayer. True prayer is not *talking* to God but *listening* to God in silence, stillness. What can the creature, man, tell the creator, God?

In essence an individual is realizing "Peace, Be Still" when the human mind ceases entertaining never-ending thoughts. Peace is always closer than one's breathing, nearer than hands and feet. Peace says to us, "Behold, *I* stand at the door and knock." Learn to develop an attitude of awareness instead of reacting with resentment and anger. "I want you to change what you said so that I can feel good," so that I can get rid of this negative feeling of resentment and anger, is essentially what the ego demands. Understanding is needed here, not for *you* to change, but *me*. We have all heard of anger management endeavors, but how in the world can you manage anger when you are caught up in that firestorm emotion of anger? We have assisted many individuals to understand and practice "Anger Avoidance." One can use the same awareness practice to let go of anger and also avoid the experience of that self-destructive emotion in the future. Until you learn to stop passing judgment on the behavior of others or certain conditions, you will continue to experience the energy of resentment welling up within you, that oft times leads to anger and sometimes violence. How does one not judge? First of all, why do we judge? The false self or ego has accepted or set a certain standard of perfection in the mind and when it perceives or judges that this standard of perfection has been violated there is the reaction of resentment and anger or hurt.

Here's where the practice of awareness comes in. There are five two-letter words you are encouraged to say within yourself (audibly, if you prefer): *"It Is As It Is."* Simply become aware of, *"she said what she said; he did what he did."* The moment you pass judgement and write a story about what was said, done or about a situation, you can observe (be aware of), that energy of resentment or hurt begins to arise within. The moment you observe that resentful feeling, it will begin to subside. It cannot withstand observation or awareness of it.

The ego, a thought form of fear, your false self, always wants to be right. It perceives itself as dying if it is wrong. Let it die! How? By practicing awareness!

This false self is sometimes called the devil in religious circles. It cannot withstand the light of truth. This is why the Master Teacher said to the Tempter, "Get thee behind me." What do you know that is behind you as you face the sunlight in early morning or late evening? Your *shadow,* of course! A shadow is not real, it has no power. So tempter is as a shadow when one faces the light of Truth. Simply acknowledge the shadow with *"it is as it is,"* but know fully that it is a shadow without any power, unless one gives it the illusion of power by writing a story about it in the mind and resisting it or feeling hurt and pain.

"Resist Not Evil" lest you lend power to it. Remember, *"it is as it is,"* without judgement, is a sure way to avoid hurt or anger. Drop all judgement and expectation and behold *IS.* You can apply the same principle to any past experience that still elicits the energy of resentment – remember, "Yesterday ended last night." As Omar the poet put it: "The moving finger writes and having writ moves on; all of your piety and wit will not lure it back to cancel half a line, nor all your tears wash out one word of it." St. Paul said in his writing, "I count not that I have apprehended, but this one thing I do, *forgetting* those things that are past." Again, "Yesterday ended last night." One or two minutes ago is as yesterday, the past!

We all do the best we understand in the state of mind that we are in at the moment we do or say whatever. Some will say, "if I were you, I would have done or said such and such." Be clear, if you were me, you would have behaved the same as I did, for you would have been in the same state of mind that dictated that behavior. So why do we judge others? The false self, the ego, thrives on finding fault and/or creating chaos in the world of humanity.

If the "System" were truly interested in rehabilitation instead of making a profit and/or punishment, it would show those incarcerated individuals a pathway to inner peace. That is what these individuals were seeking that showed forth as the behavior that violated the systems' rules of conduct. They were seeking fulfillment, peace outside of themselves; not understanding that peace is to be found within. St. Augustine said, "I sought thee at a distance and did not know that thou was near; I sought thee abroad and behold thou was within me."

15

MY WORD, MY WORLD

It is a mystery to many why their life experiences are as they are. Much time is spent pondering this or similar questions, often assuming that other people have manipulated them to be having the experiences they have. Great news for those yet unaware that the substance that constitutes one's experiences is a non-material or spiritual essence, that shows forth as a principle of certainty, just as what is happening in the tree in the middle of winter in Chicago, shows forth as abundant leaves and fruit in season. In the human scene much effort is put into changing certain experiences one is having, only to have the same or similar ones in the future. This is because of the erroneous belief that our experiences come to us in a haphazard fashion from the world of experiences outside of us. Our life experiences, in truth, are an out-picturing of our individual state of conscious-ness. Psalm 127, begins thusly: "unless the Lord build the house, they labour in vain that build it." To change experiences, a transformation of consciousness (the Lord) is necessary to realize change. The "house" is experience!

The lies that are fed to humans beings have caused such mass hypnosis that the peace is hidden under a vast array of belief systems (BS). The infinite truth is within every visible thing. The mind, however, is caught up in concepts. The search for peace begins as the concepts are shattered and Truth, God, is realized. God constitutes all things visible, including the over seven-billion humans that populate the earth. As individuals awaken to that spark of divinity within, one begins to be aware, know and understand the oneness of the Universe. "Awake thou that sleepeth!" Your True Identity is so close that the Master Teacher said, "I and my father is one." There is no separation between God and Self – True Self.

The personal sense of self is the hypnosis; the *"I"* that has a birthday, career, favorite food, etc. When you understand your own True Identity you begin to strip away the mask on your eyes that has concealed the truth of being; the result of generations of human conditioning.

It matters not how many words read or written, the awakening to that peace that surpasses human understanding must come from within. Words serve as pointers, pointing the way, but you must go the way; much like a map.

As more individuals awaken to the Truth of Being, the ripple effect will contribute toward there being peace on earth, for then, the appearance of so-called enemies will dissolve into the nothingness of its nature. The personal sense of *I* is also dissolved in the recognition of the impersonal I, the one-Self of all apparent individuals. One cannot reach a joyous ending on an unhappy journey. Worry and well-being are opposite vibrations or words to manifest as experience in one's world. Well-being cannot come when in a feeling place of worry or anxiety about the future.

Stop seeking happiness and allow joy to express itself. Happiness is an outside job, it depends on experiences that one has. Joy comes from within. "She said this, I was so happy. She said that, I was unhappy. I was promoted, I was so happy. I was fired, I was unhappy." *Haply,* means by chance, haphazard. To be happy is temporary, but joy can be permanent, for it is experienced from an attitude of gratitude. Gratitude is the expressway to joy. Whatever is entertained in consciousness is out-pictured as experience.

Many are consumed in seeking what they seem not to have, having little or no gratitude for what they *do* have. A new beginning is the *Now* moment. An awareness of Now with an attitude of gratitude reveals peace that is always at the door, knocking. This state of being dissolves that false sense of separation from the Creator, your True Identity. I and my father are one. My thoughts arise from my state of consciousness. My thoughts build a world around them. My *word* becomes my *wor(l)d* of experience. There are synonyms for *word* (idea, feeling, thought, belief system, habit, faith, fear, expectations, conditioning, tradition, etc.). There is an "L" of difference between my *word* and my *wor(l)d.* The world of experience is unique to the individual in many forms; e.g., circumstance and condition, finance, health, relationships, etc. That "L" we can say represents love. Love is the invisible law that transmutes my word into my world. We release our word and experience our world or demonstration. The word is made flesh and dwells among us. In the beginning is the word and the word is made manifest. Let us

17

make that word one of peace. It shall dwell among us. To repeat, an attitude of gratitude facilitates joyful experiences.

ATTAINING THE PEACE OF *I*

What did you call yourself before your parents were born? *"I."* Be clear on the essence of the impersonal I. We have two eyes on our face for physical vision and we have two "I's" in our very existence. As previously mentioned, the personal sense of "I" sees individual being as separate and apart from each other. The impersonal "I" that knows oneness, is that which will never leave you nor forsake you. That "I" of you existed before you entered your mother's womb. "Before Abraham was, *I AM."* I Am <u>That</u> I Am. This "I" was never born and can never die. The personal sense of "I" shall end in what is commonly called death.

We share with those who experience what is called a "loss of a loved one" in this
3-dimensional plane of humanhood, that life was never born and can never die.

Everything that has form is temporary; the ant, elephant, trees, body, etc. We must learn to look not at what is seen, but focus attention on the unseen expressing *as* tree or body; you cannot see that. That is the impersonal "I" within all form. Those on the spiritual path of awakening to their True Identity must learn to look not at what is seen, but focus attention on the unseen Reality, which is not temporary, but eternal. It matters not how long a lie has been told or believed, it is still a lie. Whatever "authority figure" perpetuates the myth, it is still a lie. Ignorance of truth does not change it. "You know what they say" is how lies of tradition or culture are often presented. *"They"* who? Have you ever dared ask yourself why you believe some of your core beliefs? Who told me what I believe? Each individual must learn to listen from within. This is not to suggest that you set yourself aside from society, but learn to "be in the world but not *of* the world" in order to find the missing peace. Silencing of thought is necessary to approach that secret place of high degree of consciousness, "If I be lifted up." The mind of "I" transforms the caterpillar to a butterfly. All in silence, you were transformed from an embryo to infant, child, teenager to adulthood, all in silence by the impersonal "I." This is the word of God being made manifest.

Many have been told that God's word is contained in a book. No one can capture God's word in a book. God's word is within everything, all form and experience. We must learn to listen from within to the silence. Speak Lord, thy Servant is listening. That Something, "I" within, knows all things. There is a difference in hearing something and listening. You may hear a car horn blowing, but listening is with your heart (spirit), not with your ears.

DROP YOUR NET OF GETTING, TO LETTING

In the world of human experience, much effort is spent chasing after things such as money, health, fulfilling relationships, love, etc. When these things seem to be lacking, people are in a state of mind usually called unhappy and sometimes depressed. They want to acquire this, that or another thing. They want to get what seems to be missing. This state of existence is anything but peaceful and one usually continues to seek that which one believes would make one happy. This is a spiritual Universe, and a lack of understanding (ignorance) of this truth does not dissolve the reality of it. The universe is governed by principles or spiritual laws. Not to be in harmony with these principles is the cause of all human suffering. Just as a violation of mathematic laws or principles brings on a result of error, ignoring the principle of gravity, if you can't fly, brings disastrous results. We pay the penalty of ignorance (ignoring principle.) As one grows in understanding of the principle that governs a concern, one becomes more at peace. The airplane pilot is at peace in the cockpit flying the jet, for he is in harmony with the principles of aerodynamics governing that flight.

As we grow in consciousness of that inner presence that governs life experiences and be aware, know and understand that we are individual expressions of this principle of abundance, we become peaceful in the realization that It knows our needs better than the human mind. Therefore, seek first to acquaint yourself with that Source and all necessary things will appear.

The clamoring and desires to acquire or capture *things* in the world can be like unto a fisherman's endeavor to capture fish with the fisherman's net. You are being encouraged to drop your net of never-ending desires and turn within where peace abides. The principle of abundance provided all substance necessary to bring you from the embryo in your mother's womb through all the different stages to the physical size and level of understanding that you are now. All of this has taken place from within your own being in silence, by an activity of Grace. You are not separate and apart from this inner presence now and never shall be. My Mentor, S.B. Fuller, talked about five major appetites by which humans are tempted. Some become addicted to one or more of these temptations that can be neutralized or overcome by the transforming power of awareness of one's True Identity. Among the appetites, that have become addicting to some, is the sex appetite. There is, of course, the inner urge of all adult males and females of all species to be attracted to each other. This is how the species is propagated and continued. The constant craving, for the sensation that sexual activity brings, is in violation of natural laws or principles of attraction between male and female. Some results of this addiction are registered in the world as incarceration in prison for rape, sexually transmitted disease, unwanted pregnancies conceived not in love between individuals, but sex addiction. Peace is covered by the constant seeking for a "piece" of sexual contact, oft times through prostitution or incest. Constant sex craving, leads many to activity of self-stimulation or masturbation. The constant dissipation of sexual energy curtails untold amounts of creativity through sex transmutation. Napoleon Hill goes into the subject of sexual transmutation in his classic book: *Think and Grow Rich.*

Learn to live by "Grace." Whatever is needed for our fulfillment already exists, so, "Let there be Light" or whatever, by an activity of Grace that brings all things visible from the invisible. "Thy Grace is my Sufficiency in all Things."

When Living by Grace, one will drop the net of cravings for anything in the external world of form and experience. A greed appetite is another form of craving that can lead to a constant feeling of dissatisfaction. Always wanting to win something, steal something that was not earned. Some have lost homes, marriages or more because of greed. Many in the government and corporate world have fallen in disgrace due to the malady of greed, leading to consequences of greater separation from that which they were seeking, a false sense of peace. Gambling casinos take in billions of dollars because of this wide spread addiction to greed. Most state governments have introduced the lottery as a means of funding education and other State Government expenses. The Jones boys grew very financially wealthy with the "numbers" game. The government called it an illegal racket at that time, before governments across America made it legal by naming it the lottery.

You can drop that net of greed by acquainting yourself with your True Identity; by learning to be still and listening to your inner voice. Fuller called the stomach appetite that which causes people to overeat and/or consume non-nutritious foods. There is a fine line of difference between filling the normal needs of the body and gratifying the ego's need to escape by overeating.

Included in this type of addiction are addicting drugs, alcohol, smoking, heroin, cocaine, etc. The craving for these substances may seem to have power, but this seeming can be unmasked in the moment of awakening to one's True Identity, by learning to still the mind. That craving is from your false self or ego. It is as a shadow, without any power. "Get thee behind me," for you are as a shadow, as I face light of truth, the light of peace – Now.

The religious or spiritual appetite causes many to become what are called religious fanatics. These people search far and wide for salvation, not realizing the truth of what the Master Teacher teaches; the kingdom of peace is within you, not outside in any holy temple. Yes, the holy temple may assist in awakening to the truth of individual beings – which is oneness with the Creator. When the individual learns to step aside, so to speak, and observe, be aware of the cravings and appetites, then one will begin to see that the craving is separate and apart from the observer. That which is observing, being aware, is one's True Identity, the real *"I"* of you. It, *"I,"* has never been addicted nor can it ever be addicted. It is a part of that all-powerful universal mind that is known by many names, God, Allah, Yahweh, Jehovah, etc. One will then have a brief glimpse of that peace that surpasses human understanding. But when you identify with "me, my and mine," you will experience fear of losing or not gaining more and more of that which you crave or that to which you are addicted. Peace you cannot find with your mind.

GIFTS AND TALENTS

Everyone on earth has fingerprints that are unlike any others of the eight-to-nine billion people that exist on the planet. The source of creation is infinite in its nature of expressing Itself in unlimited varieties of form and experience. Although it appears to human sense to be different, the essence or substance is one and the same, Spirit *As*.

This knowledge and understanding leads to a sort of testimony worth being aware of. "I will never leave you nor forsake you." Within each of us lies a unique spark of Divinity that must be found by the individual acknowledging Its presence. A recognition of that inner presence brings a peace that words are inadequate to describe.

The challenge that must be overcome is the early programming and conditioning by the outside world of "Authority" figures that would have you under control and ready to fight and die for an idea that is not yours. Many spend years at a job they do not enjoy or like. This is a source of much depression and unhappiness that leads to conflict in human relationships because they are already unhappy with themselves. If individuals were not mentally lazy, one would become awakened to the needs of others and position themselves to be of service, thereby activating the unique gift or talent for which we come into the world.

Society, in general, has become overly dependent on big business and big government for one's desires and needs. This insecure feeling adds onto anxiety, worry and other emotions that cover the inner peace awaiting recognition. There may be an apparent shortage of jobs, but there never is a shortage of work. "Work is love made visible." — Kahlil Gibran

I am reminded of Mary, who in my early years of dentistry, came and volunteered to work in the office for no pay. She made herself so useful and valuable that I was compelled to hire her as a dental assistant. Mary worked in that trusted position for over 32 years. She gave of her gifts and talents. If one is unemployed, volunteer one's self to use the gift of energy God is supplying. "Go

22

into the vineyard and work and what is right 'I' (God) will pay."
(Matthew 20:4) Some of the requirements to be awakened to your
unique purpose for being is to learn how to shut the mind off from
so much thinking and thoughts. This is the gateway to what is
called meditation, true prayer. A listening attitude is true prayer.
What can a creature tell or inform the Creator? I am aware that
many religious people disagree with the preceding statement for
the express purpose of maintaining discipline or control of the
masses. The focus must be to "open out a way for that imprisoned
splendor to escape," as Browning puts it. That imprisoned splendor
is your True Identity, your Spiritual Self which is always closer
than breathing, nearer than hands and feet. That inner presence is
always within, awaiting one's recognition which activates *IT*.
Now, the momentum of habit of thinking and entertaining thoughts
is deeply ingrained in humanhood, but one who is sincere will
practice being aware, being a beholder without reacting to things,
events, people or situations. "It is as it is," is the mantra of one
who is not thinking or talking themselves. "Be in the world, but not
of the world." Keep your mind and thoughts off of this world and
become aware of the inner presence which, again, is your True
Identity. There peace is discovered; (*dis*-covered or uncovered).

By the activity of grace your gifts and talents will be
revealed to you. You will then be transformed in consciousness,
much the same as the caterpillar becomes the butterfly.

Once you understand who *"I"* is, you will never be the
same; peace will be your home station.

No one need prepare to meet God; you are meeting God
every *Now Moment*, every day. Release the past and live Now. To
free the personal human self of worry, anxiety, judging others or
any mental place that displaces peace, you must know the truth of
your True Identity, your spiritual identity of *I;* ye shall know the
truth and the truth shall make you free of all maladies of
humanhood.

These words you are reading or any others that you hear or
read will not of themselves alter your state of consciousness. But
the words imparted from within your own being when the mind is
silent of thinking and thoughts, then a transformation of
consciousness takes place and peace is realized.

The supreme purpose of being in this three-dimensional plane of humanhood is to wake up from the mass hypnosis of humanity; just as with breathing, no one can do it for you.

ANY OF MANY

No matter how many peace treaties are signed in the world of humanhood, they are temporary at best and often not worth the paper they are written on. Real peace is individually realized when and as one awakens to the True Identity of one's being; then fulfillment is found. In the world are many paths that deceive and lead astray the ones who are ignorant of the truth of being. The conditioning that begins in utero, before birth, due to the mother's diet of food and thought, passes to the unborn child, for the two are one.

After birth those Giants in the child's life known as parents are the first "authority" figures that begin the conditioning or hypnosis process that often lasts a lifetime until there is a dissatisfaction with life experiences and one becomes open and receptive to that within-ness that always knocks at the door of consciousness. "Behold, I stand at the door and knock." (Rev. 3:20)

I recall in my early years of following tradition in my rural community in Arkansas, of going to the Mourner's Bench to "get religion" to prepare myself to meet God. No one told me, nor did I understand, that I was already meeting God every day, as are all the plants, animals and people of the world. "They" were the authority image before me, therefore, I followed tradition and followed the belief rituals as expected of me. The Mourner's Bench was the tradition of belief in many southern states at that time.

This path is followed by many people in the world today. The "Mourner's Bench" syndrome was mainly a tradition in the southern part of the United States, instituted in large part by the slaveholders. There remains the question if the slaveholder would volunteer to teach the slaves anything that would empower the slaves? No! Once the momentum of habit is established it is self-governed until a light of truth enters the consciousness of a sufficient number of individuals to make a difference. "Ten righteous men can save a City." This type of programming is done in so many aspects of humanhood that it becomes accepted as the right thing to do. So, when I visited a church in Pittsburg, PA, while serving in the U.S. Army, I felt it was wrong to allow young people to become members of that church without first going to the "Mourner's Bench."

Whatever path that has been travelled, to take an individual away from the center of peace within, will be dissolved and vanish as the truth of being is acknowledged. This recognition cannot be done intellectually with the mind. As one man put it, "Einstein will miss it, but Bozo will get it," for it must be discerned from within your own consciousness and not intellect. We are admonished in biblical scripture "to take no thought for your life, but seek ye first the kingdom" and whatever is needed to establish one in peace shall appear.

The constant or chronic feeling that this moment is incomplete, something other than "what is" is needed to experience happiness, is the nature of humanhood and its conditioning. We can come to understand how to rise above that programming. Learn to still the mind of thoughts and thinking. We were given dominion over the mind by our Creator.

To establish the habit of reacting to other people's behavior is a sure way to not be at peace. Know well that you cannot write a script for the behavior of others. Whatever they do or say, remember those five two-letter words, "It is as it is;" then do not pass judgement and write a story of the behavior such as, "that's crazy," "they are disrespecting me," "I'm sick and tired of him," etc. You will then react to the story that you write. No one makes you angry except your false self, the ego, what you say to yourself. We call it MSU, "making stuff up," in your mind and then reacting to what the ego made up.

COMMUNICATE, COOPERATE, COORDINATE = SUCCESS

Much human conflict, misunderstanding and frustration are experienced in the world because of the inability of people to work together harmoniously. This is due, in large part, to the ego asserting itself. Remember, ego is a word to describe the false

25

sense of self. This is an illusion of self that can never be real. Another term used by the religious community is "devil." "The devil did it," they say. The ego loves drama and confusion; if it cannot find it already existing, it will create its own. This is what keeps it seemingly alive. In reality it has only an illusion of life, not real. It thrives where there is ignorance of the True Identity of one's being.

There is much concern in many communities across the United States about the so-called "gang problem." These groups form for survival purposes. Here and there is a young man whose parents no longer support him financially, he cannot find a job, he is broke. He turns to the attraction of what he is told is fast or easy money. The adult citizens of the community criticize his behavior, not realizing that what they are witnessing is a direct result of seeds planted by the community. The community has not learned to work together to build businesses that would not only provide jobs for such a young person but also present an image of what he can *do* and *be* as an adult.

The lack in many communities of businesses as an image for the young people is principally due to a lack of understanding of how to work together. People who do *not* live in the community see the opportunity and seize it by operating most of the businesses and taking millions of dollars out of circulation. Money is to a community as blood is to the body. If blood does not circulate in the hand or any organ of the body, that part of the body dies. If money fails to circulate, the community suffers or dies.

Where ever there are two or more people in any endeavor, to realize or experience success in a project, there are 3 C's of social skills that are necessary. As Dinah Washington sang, "starting with the ABC's of it, right down to the XYZ of it, help me understand the mystery of it," and the mystery is how to work together by practicing the 3 C's of Communication, Cooperation and Coordination. One must get beyond ego and confess one's ignorance in the practical understanding of the 3 C's.

The first C is *Communication*. You and I could never *Cooperate,* which is the second C, if we do not know how to communicate. A lack of communication is wide spread in many communities due to ego-based self-talk. As an example, if I am thinking of what I am going to say, while you are yet speaking, or try to talk over your words, then I am not listening. Listening is an integral part of effective communication. There must be a deep silence of thoughts for one to really listen. In that silence words of response are offered from within to facilitate effective communication.

It has been said, "To go fast, go alone; to go far, go together." Cooperation is essential to building a business. Many people in communities of high unemployment will cooperate in non-profit ventures but not in profit-making business ventures. This mind-set is passed from generation to generation.

These are usually the same people that play the role of being a victim of outside forces, rarely assuming responsibility for a situation or condition. As within, so without – as experience.

The ego always feels that it is right regardless of outcome. To be wrong for the ego is to die, so it struggles to stay alive from its perspective.

As has been stated, however, that sense of being alive is illusionary at best, but never real. To confess that you don't know how to communicate and cooperate is the primary step to learning those basic steps to stem the tide of unemployment and violence that often accompanies it in urban communities. Those so-called small Mom-and-Pop stores that appear to be successful in the urban communities are run by people who do not live in the community. You can bet your bottom dollar that they are effectively communicating, cooperating and coordinating those individuals who are operating the business. This translates into success.

I mention these things here because an absence of Peace in the community and the individual has its origin in ignorance of how to work together. A final word about communication, which is difficult to realize if one or more persons already have a prejudiced idea about the topic discussed: One is usually hearing another point of view through the screen of that pre-established or prejudiced idea. That person is *hearing* but not *listening*. You can hear a radio, for example, but not be listening. To listen, you must be consciously aware of what is being offered by others. You hear with your ears and auditory faculties, while you listen with your heart or spirit. Listening know-how is a gift that is developed by practice. The ego of an individual is so busy thinking and entertaining thoughts, that listening is foreign to it. The ego, your false sense of self, is busy reacting to the information fed to it by one or more of the five senses. This personal sense of self, ego, is occupied by judging others as right, wrong, pretty, ugly, disrespectful, or whatever its belief system governs it to judge.

NON-REACTION, BE A BEHOLDER

Your mind, in its most effective usage, is a clear transparency for the inner Light, your God Self, to use to impart Truth messages as the "still, small voice." As an analogy, a clean window pane is a transparency for sunlight, the sunlight comes *through* the window pane not *from* the window pane. If, however, there is mud on the window pane, the sunlight would be blocked and could not come through. In a similar sense, if there's mud on the mind in the form of beliefs or thoughts, that Inner Light cannot impart its direction, government or information to you or the individual. "Be Still" is the command to the mind that is constantly reacting to the temptation of the world. Whether those tempters are persons, situations, or conditions, non-reaction can be developed in order for peace to abide. Peace is not something to *Get*, it is something to *Let*. "Behold, I stand at the door and knock." (Rev. 3:20) Open the door and *let* peace and understanding come in through a transparent mind that listens from within.

You may be called cold, callous or indifferent as you learn non-reaction to the things and events of the World, but be encouraged to "be in the world, but not of the world," traditions and customs. One must become aware, know and understand that life is immortal or eternal; Life was never born nor can Life ever die. Life is God. In truth, there is no such thing as "my life" or "your life." There is *one* Life, "God's Life," individualized *as* an infinite variety of forms. All forms are temporary. That tree outside, one day will not be there, but that which is expressing itself *as* tree, you cannot see that: That's Life! Give your attention to what is not seen. Paul, in 2 Cor. 4:18, tells us, "While we look not at the things which are seen (visible), but at the things which are not seen (invisible), for the things which are seen are temporal while the things which are not seen are eternal." All forms are temporary whether it be plant, animal, mineral, self or a loved one.

In our human existence, there is often grief and sadness at the loss of a family member or loved one. When this experience occurs, you are encouraged to take an extra dose of gratitude. Sadness cannot sustain itself where an attitude of gratitude exists; feeling grateful for having known and shared the time together, for having a memory to recall past experiences and for feeling their presence even now. Remember *"I"* as your True Identity and theirs. You will react less and act more in harmony with the principle of Divine Grace.

To know and understand this principle is to be aware without reacting. All things and events come and pass. All through scripture we find these words: "and it came to pass." So let it pass without reacting, thereby dwell in peace. Peace is "the secret place of the most high" state of consciousness. To know and experience God, dwell in that secret place. In that state there is no reacting to the things of this world of humanhood. Know the truth that this is an all-spiritual universe, there is no spot where God is not. Judge not from appearances for they will deceive and mislead you. Appearances inform the human mind of what is real and train it to react to those appearances. This *inform*-ation steals peace and joy from the individual and produces an information overload to the ego.

The behavior of other people is a source of much unhappiness for many individuals; what someone did or said. The more one uses the emotion of reacting (which comes from passing judgement) the more that things, events or circumstances will appear in one's experience to initiate reaction. A rise in consciousness will lead one "to see" further, to understand clearer, that this is indeed an all-spiritual universe. "If *I* be lifted up:" *I* is consciousness individualized as you, me and everyone. Where ever we may be *I*, the Christ consciousness, is always within us. Intense reaction to another person's behavior is often magnified in personal relationships. Use the exercise in being aware (see "Anger Avoidance," pg 121) to dissolve these conflicts.

You are encouraged to become alert to when you are passing judgment on your husband, wife, friend or whomever. Begin to be aware of that energy of resentment as it begins to well up in your feeling nature. As you step aside, so to speak, and observe that energy of resentment inside of you, it will immediately begin to abate, subside. It cannot withstand being observed because it is not real.

Practice communicating to the other individual how you *"feel"* when he or she behaves (say or do) in the manner that is causing a reaction in you. Be alert to not begin your communication with "you," but with "I feel ___ when ___." You see, there could have been a misinterpretation of the behavior. "How do you feel about _____?" is a bridge to more effective communication. To be human is to make mistakes and errors in judgement and behavior. To understand the oneness of the universe will not only neutralize many interpersonal conflicts but also contribute to bringing peace on earth by a ripple effect.

As one begins to awaken to his or her True Identity as being a spiritual being and recognizes that same identity in others, we learn that there is only one's self to forgive for having seen another as anything other than spiritual – although *they* may be still ignorant of it, my assignment is to stay home in that understanding.

What seems to separate us is the universal human belief system of good and evil. It is then that individuals become as a branch separated from the tree. To become separated in consciousness from the source of all good, peace and joy is to be as the Prodigal Son who uses up his substance. But as with that lost son, we can individually always return to the Father's house and cease having a banquet with the swine. (Luke 15:11) This is commonly referred to as the prodigal son. Cease the prodigal experience; wake up!

Conscious awareness of the Truth of Being establishes anyone in peace that surpasses human understanding. Become as a clear window pane and let the inner light lead and guide. It will go before you and make the crooked places straight and you shall dwell in the house of peace forever; reacting will be a thing of the past. Know well that emotional reaction of resentment is wasted effort and only adds more layers of frustration and confusion that displace peace; simply learn from any mistakes, pick yourself up and start again by listening to your inner guidance.

AMAZING GRACE

All things visible had their origin in the invisible, *all* things. Mentally visit your favorite grocery store or supermarket. Notice all the fruits and vegetables; the green, red, yellow and brown colors. Can you see in your mind's eye the multitude of shapes and sizes?

Take note of the many canned foods on the shelves. Visit the meat section and take note of the variety of choices. Now, this is only one store. Just think of how many other stores and supermarkets there are in your town or city. What about state, country, other countries on earth? Everything visible emanates out of the invisible realm of existence; mineral, plants and animals, including you and me and all other eight or nine billion people on earth, not to mention other planets in the universe.

This invisible Source of all that is visible has not been diminished in the least. There is a power, wisdom and intelligence, beyond human understanding, that brings forth Itself as the infinite forms, varieties and experiences that we call Grace. By the activity and power of Grace, all things visible appear in the world, yet all things that do appear are temporal or temporary. Remember 2 Cor. 4:18 where it is written, "we look not at that which are seen (visible), but at the things unseen" (God is invisible); "for the things which are seen are temporal, but the things which are not seen are eternal." To "look" is to give attention to, focus on. Are you seeking peace and *fulfillment?* Give your attention to that which is invisible. As I, you or anyone, acknowledge *It* in all our ways, *It* shall direct our path of action and thinking.

Though mankind cannot create anything, he is so quick to claim "my land, my country, my oil or my whatever." This state of mind lacks the understanding of "The earth is the Lord's and the fullness thereof." (Psalm 24:1) There is abundance in the seen and unseen realms of the universe. Supply is infinite and invisible. Man's ignorance and greed lead to what is experienced on earth as war, lack, poverty and scarcity and the seeming absence of peace within individuals. Ego-driven "leadership" has led to the hypnosis of humanity in general.

Humanhood seems to be driven to get more and more of things. Let us begin to turn within to the invisible realm and the "things" shall appear as needed. Seek first the source and substance of all things, i.e., Spirit, *that* the world knows not.

Amazing Grace brought you and me from the union of a sperm and egg (that no human knows how to make) to all stages of mental and physical growth that we have attained. This Source and Substance is known by many names; God, Allah, Christ, Jehovah, Yahweh. By whatever name it is called does not alter its nature of unlimited abundance and amazing grace. This Source reveals itself as ideas that we humans call inventions.

From where did the idea of man's ability to fly through the sky come? The principle of aeronautics has always existed, just as the principle of mathematics and gravity has always existed. Man's understanding of them came through a transparent mind that was listening to that "still, small voice" within. This Source is the voice within us all, but few understand how to still the mind of thinking thoughts in order to listen to that inner presence that says in essence, "behold I stand at the door and knock."

New levels of understanding can be reached in the light of freely given grace of Source. By the constant activity and power of Grace, untold numbers of other revelations or inventions remain to appear in the world just as the internet, television, cell phone, etc. Supply is infinite. Supply is not the form but is the *substance* of the form, what the form is constituted of, Spiritual Substance. Just as you cannot separate the desk from the oakwood that constitutes the desk, the wood and desk *is* one. Just as I and my Father (Source) *is* one.

By Grace is the gift of life given to us. We are not separate and apart from that Source of life, maybe just unaware of the oneness of us all. Global unity already exists; however, a lack of understanding – ignorance – causes anxiety, tension and lack of peace. "Awake, thou that sleepeth" to eliminate personal conflict and wars.

I cannot breathe for you, neither can you digest food for me; it is an individual activity. So is the awakening process from the mass hypnosis of the world of humanity. We are encouraged to be *in* the world but not be *of* the world. Many people use a multiplicity of words in an appeal to a God somewhere to change an evil condition or person; true prayer is not *talking* to God, but *listening* to that "still, small voice" uttered from within by Grace.

Living by Grace, we must learn to still the mind of thoughts and thinking and know that *"I* will be with you always, even until the end of the world."

Dropping the net of human concerns is necessary for the Grace to appear as perfect peace. The "still, small voice" from within may be an impulse or inner urge and not an audible voice one hears. Anyone can transform from a habitual pattern of stress and inharmony to the personal experience of peace and joy which is the antidote for these maladies.

Amazing grace is the conduit for this transformation and only God knows the mystery of it. "Man does not live by bread (things) alone, but by every word that proceeds from the mouth of God." (Matt. 4:4) The mouth of God is Silence of human thinking.

THE MIRACLE OF PEACE

It is only humans that are not at peace. Everything in the universe that is governed by a principle is at peace. A principle is truth or law that cannot be repealed, amended or modified in any way. If anything is done by principle one time and a particular result is obtained, that same result is available across the world. It does not make a difference if that result is obtained by deliberate intent by an individual who is listening from within or by what appears to human consciousness as an "accidental" discovery. This so-called "accident" is simply spirit revealing itself to human consciousness, this world.

Peace is already established, therefore we might as well put up the sword in an attempt to establish peace. God is the same today as God always has been. Any attempt to influence God is vanity. Two times two equaling four has always existed and unlimited appealing to God will not alter that truth or principle. There is no debate in your mind if you observe someone has written two times two equaling five. In a similar sense, when we know the truth of individual beings as spiritual, we look beyond the appearance of evil knowing the truth about him or her. In doing so, we do not empower an illusion or human concept and remain at peace.

To awaken to your True Identity as a spiritual being, you recognize that this identity is always at peace, you are the miracle of peace in physical form. To regain knowledge and understanding of this truth is to be in the world but not of the world.

The source and substance of our existence can never be separate and apart from each of us, although to become aware of this truth, one must see through the fog of human conditioning, programming and hypnosis. As a beam of light comes into a darkened room from the sun, we know that the light is not separate and apart from the sun. In a similar sense do we exist, not separate and apart from our forever peaceful Source.

SELF-SACRIFICE

The false sense of human reality is the root cause of all inharmony experienced in the world. This false sense of self thrives and feeds off of non-peaceful relationships, conditions and situations. Again, this false sense is called ego. Someone has said ego is an acronym for "edge God out." We know, however, that the true God is omnipresent and can never be edged out, but a lack of awareness or ignorance of this truth will usher in the appearance of illusions that, to human belief systems, are real.

Let us recall someone saying, "She really made me angry." No, if anger was not a part of your makeup or consciousness, anger could not come out or be expressed. Be clear, what someone says has absolutely no power of itself to anger or upset you. It is what you say to yourself in passing judgement that causes your reaction. "That is crazy; she's disrespecting me; I'm sick and tired of her, etc." These ego-based stories that you write in your mind are the basis of the emotional reactions that are experienced. It's the story that you write in your mind *about* what someone says or does that you are reacting. In other words, once you pass judgement the energy of resentment begins to arise in you, which becomes anger and sometimes violence. As you practice the choiceless awareness of the actions of others without judging, you can observe that energy of resentment subsiding, thereby avoiding the experience of anger. Dissolve resentment by using the faculty of awareness.

There are some who play old tapes in memory of long-ago experiences and become upset again and again, as if the events are happening now.

Peace always exists where there appears to be inharmony. "Behold, I stand at the door and knock." God is the only Reality because this is an all-spiritual universe. The nature of peace cannot be described in words, it must be experienced, just as the taste of a banana must be experienced. As you learn to deny this false identity entrance into your consciousness, you will develop the ability to simply be aware that "she said what she said, he did what he did" without writing a story or judging the behavior in your mind. Whatever was said or done is now in the past, a part of history that cannot be erased. The past does not exist unless one supports it with current thoughts. As Omar, the poet, wrote, "The moving finger writes, and having writ, moves on; all of your piety and wit will not lure it back to cancel half a line; nor all your tears wash out one word of it." Yesterday ended last night. St. Paul wrote, "I count not that I have apprehended, but this one thing I do, *forgetting* that which is behind me." The record written, must stand but you have the eternal Now moment at hand to make choices.

I remind you, however, that the lower self, ego, does not relish *Now,* for it perceives that it will die. In order to experience peace, one must sacrifice, deny ego by living by grace in the *Now*. Let go and let God appear as whatever is needed. To recognize oneness with the Source brings the light of truth to any and all situations or problems. In this light of recognition the "earth melts," the so-called problems disappear and peace is uncovered. These are merely words and no words spoken, written, heard or read can reveal the magnificence of recognizing your True Identity within, that inner presence, *I AM.*

FLOWERS OF LIFE

The energy that is expressing itself as you and me is called by many names, depending on the culture by which one is programmed or conditioned. Some call it God, Jehovah, Allah, Yahweh, etc. Let us call it Life.

Life expresses itself in an infinite variety of forms and experiences through an activity of grace. This energy is malleable and fluid-like, taking on the form and experience for individual human beings according to the state of consciousness one maintains. In order to initiate conception for a certain effect or result, according to a law or principle governing that particular sequence of activity (giving birth to the effect or result) one must listen from within. The thoughts and behavior of an individual arise out of the level of consciousness of that individual. To endeavor to change experiences without a change or transformation of consciousness is an exercise in futility. "Unless the Lord builds the house they labor in vain that build." (Psalm 127) The Lord is the individual's own consciousness. The house is one's experience.

This energy that shows forth or manifests itself as form and experience in an individual's world is an out-picturing of individual or collective consciousness of a society of people; as within, so without. An apple is an apple throughout; not a radish inside. This life energy flows according to the pattern it receives from thought and belief system operating. We flow that energy usually out of ignorance. Whether with deliberate intent through planning or ignorance, we are the *flow*-ers of this energy which is life substance. That is why this section is called "flowers of life" in a light-hearted attempt to get your attention.

Life experiences consist of a series of choices we make. No one can or should protect me or you from the choices we make. Choices made will be in alignment with peace and harmony as we give attention to the inner authority of our True Identity, that which is not seen but speaks in silence from within. Do not confuse thoughts in mind with listening from within – Reality. Learn to observe, be aware of thoughts by practicing awareness of each finger on your hands. There you will note the difference in *thinking* and *awareness*. Do not move or look at the fingers, simply be aware of each, one at a time. This practice may lead you to the door of meditation, through which door you acquaint yourself with God, peace and joy.

I encourage you to realize that where ever you are on the path of peace is a good starting point. The Prince of Peace, God, is right where you are, for He is omnipresence and omnipresent; present now and everywhere. So your place is a good starting point. You start by acknowledging that you are always one with your Source, just as the ray of sunlight is one with its source, the sun.

Your Source only knows peace and perfection; therefore, those same qualities already exist within you. It may be covered by debris of thoughts and thinking that the world has taught you and the momentum of habit may seem insurmountable to subdue. In fact you, of your personal sense of self, are unable to do so because it is that same sense of self which is programmed and conditioned with the habit in the first place. Only a transformation of consciousness can effect a change of experience.

As one of my favorite authors, Joel S. Goldsmith, puts it, "Only a transformation of consciousness will produce a transformation of human experience. Never forget that. A transformation: 'be ye renewed through the transforming of your mind,' – that's the secret! When you go through a transformation of consciousness you become renewed in body ... you will make and remake your bodies and your purses and your home, and you will do it in the same way – by a transformation of consciousness. And that transformation of consciousness comes when instead of having more faith in bodies and more faith in money or more faith in demonstrations, when you release that and turn wholeheartedly to filling your consciousness with truth, *keep* your mind stayed on God, *abide* in the Word and *let* the Word abide in you, **then** you will find that that spiritual transition within will take place as a physical transition without. And **It** will change the whole mode of your living, your body, your business, your art, your profession, everything will be brought under the grace of God, instead of under the laws of matter or economics. You see that?" Goldsmith departed this plane of existence in 1964, but his teaching continues to expand and inspire millions worldwide through books and tapes under the title *The Infinite Way*.

We, as "flow-ers" of this energy called Life, do it according to the states of consciousness and not through human efforts. Again, unless the Lord build the house of experience, they labor in vain that build. The Lord is your very own consciousness. The mystery of this energy, Life, is God's alone to know, of how it transmutes substance of the invisible to visible realm of materiality. This includes our bodies and the bodies of all plants and animals. To be aware that you and I are never separate and apart from this Source energy establishes peace and joy in the depth of one's being.

All temptation to believe in a power of evil is diminished to the point of non-existence as this Source is realized. "Get thee behind me," we can say to these illusions. For as I face the light of Truth, you are as a shadow in the same sense that as I face the light of the sun, my shadow is behind me, without any power.

As in a flower garden, there are many varieties of flowers; roses, tulips, lilacs, etc. The colors are beautiful and varied as are the different smells or fragrances. We understand the energy of life is *one* within each of the many forms of flowers in the garden. In a similar sense, in the realm of humanity with infinite varieties of belief systems, ethnic groups, states and stages of consciousness development, we acknowledge the effects of flow-ers of the one energy, life, showing forth *as* forms and experiences in harmony with each individual flow-er. These forms and experiences are infinite. Limitations or finiteness do not exist because consciousness is omnipresent, infinite. Let us celebrate the diversity of humanity in lieu of being a source of conflict and wars.

The human mind, with its limitations, has incessant judgements and opinions that cause it to not be at peace. This state of flux and chaos in the collective consciousness of billions of people is out-pictured as problems and chaos in the world. Nevertheless, though chaos may exist all around you, it need not come near your dwelling place of peace and serenity. "Let there be peace on earth, and let it begin with me."

That peace is uncovered and experienced by a conscious recognition of the presence of God within as the source and substance of your very being. You are not separate and apart from It at any time.

THE SECRET PEACE PLACE

Take a pen or pencil and write, not print, the two words, "Peace Place." Note that depending on how large or small the second letter in each word is written, one word can become the other. You will have to die to your old way of thinking in order to move to or experience this peace place. As Paul said in his writing, "I die daily;" you must die to those egotistical cravings that are based on pride of possession or recognition, die to the habit of passing judgment of good and evil, and come to know and understand the spiritual oneness of the universe, without exception.

That place of peace is not dependent on time nor space, but on he that dwells in the secret place of the most high consciousness. Many people change cities or states hoping to find peace somewhere other than where they presently reside. Peace is not dependent on *where* you are being, but *who* you are being. Where ever you may go in the world, you take you with *you,* your own state of consciousness. It's not in the *land,* but in the *man,* the individual who dwells in the secret place of a high state of consciousness and abides in the shadow of Its unfoldment. Few individuals there be that find this place, although It is available to everyone who enters into awareness, Silence. It is a place of Silence that is independent on one's physical dwelling place. Know well, every place is beautiful in its own way, for there is not a spot where God is not. Omnipresence is the nature of God!

There is one reason that keeps an individual seeking peace and fulfillment outside of him or herself, and that is the beliefs that are held in consciousness, human consciousness. A belief will keep truth hidden, and cause all kinds of chaos in the life experience of the individual holding that belief. There are those who will tell you, "this is the way I was raised," as if "this" is the proper measure of the right path. The parents, themselves, may be victims of human beliefs and indoctrination!

How were you "raised?" Not only by those authority figures that were seen as giants when you were a child, called parents; but also by the news media last year, your friends and playmates, the tradition of culture around you? All of these are influential in shaping one's belief system (or BS). In order to rise above the human belief systems, an individual must rise in consciousness above "this world" and be aware, know and understand eternal truth, principles.

All human behavior is governed by the hypnosis of believing in the materiality of the universe; whereas, the universe is and has always been a spiritual universe. Spiritual discernment cannot be realized with the human mind. Beliefs lodge in the human mind only, and all thinking and thoughts arise out of beliefs held collectively by the human race as well as individual belief systems.

My personal behavior was erratic as long as I *believed* that someone had taken my topcoat by deliberate intent or by accident here in this Chicago winter weather. Imagine my relief when I picked up my suit and shirts from the cleaners and discovered I had inadvertently put my topcoat, with gloves in the pockets, in the cleaners also. This incident was instruction for me on how human beliefs dictate human behavior. It reminded me to free myself of fear and to live by grace. Now, grace is not something yet to come, but is a present moment activity to be recognized.

The human mind constantly compares. Wars are fought between nations based on beliefs that one nation is taking something of a material nature from the other, until a so-called peace treaty is signed after sacrificing thousands of human lives and immeasurable human suffering is caused; pure insanity.

The human mind is as a tool or instrument to be used. When the ego is very active, however, the human mind believes itself to be an entity separate and apart from everyone else and the truth of oneness is foreign to it or negated all together.

To repeat, the human mind in its most effective usage ought to be a clear transparency as is a clear window pane on a sunny day. You see, the sunlight does not come *from* the window pane, but comes *through* the window pane of glass. If, however, there is mud on the glass, the sunlight cannot come through. In a similar sense, if there are thoughts (mud) occupying the mind, it is no longer a transparency for that Inner Light or Presence to guide, direct and whisper words of peace and joy; not audible words, but a feeling to be aware of; that Presence within restores "the years the locusts have eaten" (Joel 2:25); you were lost in humanhood beliefs in the appearance of things, in the material world of the senses.

The source and substance of our very being has never left any one of us. Realizing this truth dissolves stress of ongoing experiences and we begin to live by grace instead of worry, anxiety and concern.

The experience of humanhood is somewhat akin to that of a fish out of water. We can learn how to be at ease as a fish *in* water, their natural habitat. Our natural habitat is to be aware, know and understand the nature of oneness in this spiritual universe regardless of the appearance to the senses.

There are many human concerns that trouble individuals and keep them removed from that place of peace. There are two concerns of many individuals that seem to be leading the pack in peace-busting. One of those is relationship conflict, people not getting along with each other; the other is financial insecurity.

The root cause of human conflict is that the personal sense of self is active. Very few individuals are awakened to their True Identity, true spiritual identity or impersonal self. The personal sense of self has a birthday, career, history of experiences and has accepted death as an inevitable end to life, an experience that is feared by this personal sense of life, or ego. The religious call this ego by the name, "devil."

The ego is in constant judgment of other people's behavior and readily reacts with the energy of resentment that arises within one's self after having passed judgment on another person. You see, the ego sets a standard of perfection in the mind and, when it perceives that that standard has been violated, it reacts. The tradition of the culture could be the standard of perfection the ego has accepted!

"That's crazy," "wrong," "disrespecting me," "evil," are some of the words that the ego uses in passing judgment on others. The ego has a power addiction and always wants to be and believes that it is right, no matter what the issue might be. It believes that there is power in being right every time and finds itself in frequent arguments with other ego-based individuals. The personal sense of self, the ego, believes that to be wrong on any point is equal to dying; therefore, it feels it must defend itself by arguments or even fighting.

For those individuals desiring to return to the path leading to the peace place, there must be self-sacrifice, an emptying of the personal sense of self. One does this by awakening to the impersonal Self, the True Identity of one's being. Just as darkness disappears where there is light, so does the personal sense of self abate in recognition of the inner presence of "I," the True Identity of an individual.

In this dimension of existence, human beings call themselves as individuals by the name *"I"* – "I" am hungry, "I" am at work, on the phone, etc. This is referring to the personal sense of "I." The "I" of their True Identity was never born and can never die, for it is one with the Creator. "I and my father are one" are words of the Master Teacher, Jesus, for He recognized his oneness with God, The Father. That same Divine presence is within each one of us waiting for recognition of it. "Behold, I stand at the door and knock." To open the door of individual consciousness is to uncover the missing peace.

To awaken to your True Identity of "I" will enable you to "see" the same essence in your neighbor and any so-called enemy, thereby causing interpersonal conflict and wars to no longer exist. Whereas I was blind, now I see. If "I" be lifted up, peace shall appear where stress and conflict once existed.

One may begin the practice of stilling the mind of thinking thoughts, by becoming *aware*. Thinking and awareness are akin to each other, but different.

Note that in being aware and in the ceasing of thoughts, you become attuned to the *Now*. The past, nor future is of no importance. The peace of God can only be realized in the *Now* moment.

In interpersonal relations with other people, the experience gained from practicing being aware can be invaluable. Whereas you were easy to react with resentment and anger at what others said or did, now you simply detach yourself by being *aware* that "it is as it is," "he said what he said," "she did what she did;" it is now a part of the past and of itself has absolutely no power to cause you to react with resentment nor anger.

It may be helpful to know and understand that we all *do* or *say* the best we can in the state of mind we are in at the moment of that particular behavior. That includes you and I also. Since that is apparently factual, does reasoning justify judging another person and reacting with resentment or anger? "It is as it is" – five two-letter words in your mind, supported by being consciously aware without writing a story in your mind about what another person said or did not say; what they did or did not do (their behavior). You will be able to be at peace even when all around you appears to be in chaos.

The ego of humanhood may reject these suggestions because it thrives on conflict and chaos, plus that personal sense of self always wants to be right. Self-sacrifice will be beyond the ability of most people unless unfavorable experiences become concretized and an attitude of surrender consumes the individual. Awareness is key for transformation of consciousness to a mountain-top experience of peace that is beyond human understanding. Awareness is a gateway to meditation or true prayer of contact with God, our creator. "The only form of prayer acceptable to God is absolute silence." (Joel Goldsmith)

The second widespread cause of not being at a place of peace in consciousness is lack and limitation in the human experience. While abundance of good is the nature of God's creation, individual experience of it is directly dependent on the level of conscious awareness of one's True Identity and the invisible nature of Supply.

In truth, the cause of experiencing lack and limitation in any form is rooted in ignorance, a lack of understanding of the spiritual oneness of the universe. Human experience in general is a reflection of beliefs in materiality. All material form that is visible came from the invisible realm of Spirit; hence, always is the *essence* of Spirit though it appears in infinite variety of forms.

The focus must rise from the material form of that which is desired to the essence or substance of the form. The seeming lack of supply in the form of money, for example, causes many people to chase after money. In those cases, they are not looking to *supply* but to the *form* that supply takes, money. "The love of money is the root of all evil." (1 Timothy 6:10) The source of all supply is invisible because Source is spiritual. To focus on the effect, instead of cause, is to be deluded into a sense of lack and limitation. Consciousness forms itself *as* money; it is the source and substance of it.

The substance of all form is invisible. That which appears is not made of anything that appears. "All things were made by him (Spirit), and without Him was not anything made that was made." (John 1:3) "While we look not at the things which are seen, but at the things which are not seen; for the things that are seen are temporary, but the things which are not seen are eternal." (2 Corinthians 4:18)

The five senses *inform* the mind of the material world, but this *inform*-ation is a limited horizon beyond which must be spiritually discerned, for awareness and understanding, knowing the truth makes an individual free of lack and limitation and peace is uncovered.

That freedom is a transition from a material sense of life to an understanding that the invisible is the substance of all visible forms; hence, turning to the Father of form is very practical and wise. Acknowledging this Source seems to activate it in one's life experiences. The "how" of its activity is beyond human understanding.

Whatever the call is to lead you away from that peace place, simply realize it as a temptation. As the Master Teacher taught us, all temptation is as a shadow without any power, so we, too, must say "get thee behind me" temptation, of whatever nature. For as you face the light of truth, God, you will be at peace. "Thou will keep him in perfect peace whose mind is stayed on thee, because he trusteth in thee." (Isaiah 26:3)

We can never uncover inner peace while trying to get God to do something to discords, inharmony or lack. Inner peace can only be uncovered by turning to Spirit within and realizing Spirit is the fulfillment of every need and do not resist what *appears* to be evil, for you will only empower it.

The short of it is there must be a transformation of consciousness from that of a human being to a recognition of your True Identity of a spiritual being. The source of peace is also the substance of peace. The *giver* and the *gift* is one, Spirit, God.

It is the very nature of the human mind to entertain thoughts of past experiences, good and bad experiences. Both of which obscure and cover the NOW moment of being. Peace can only be realized in the NOW, never in playing old tapes of the past in memory, nor being anxious about the future.

Through practicing awareness of the eternal NOW moment, one will find the cessation, silencing of thoughts racing through the mind, blocking the realization of omnipresent peace of *NOW.*

The discords and inharmony of the world may appear to assert themselves from outside of you, but it is only by accepting them as real that they appear inside of the mind. Stay tuned to the peace station by simply being a beholder of the events of "this world;" be *in* the world but not *of* the world by practicing awareness, without judgment.

Do not mingle observation with the emotion of labeling something good or bad. To successfully be a beholder, you must, as Emerson says, "get your bloated nothingness out of the way." It is the ego, your false sense of self, that is emotionally upset, worried or anxious. As an individual rises in conscious awareness, this state of mind dissolves, just as darkness disappears in the presence of light.

There is the story that the sun overheard talk of darkness existing somewhere. The sun searched for this place of darkness but could never find it, for where ever the sun went it took its light with it. So with an individual; if you are at peace, it doesn't matter that the outside world appears chaotic.

The Peace Song, written by Jill Jackson, expresses the beauty of this state of being:

"Let there be peace on earth, and let it begin with me. Let there be peace on earth, the peace that was meant to be. With God as our Father, family all are we. Let me walk with my family, in perfect harmony. Let peace begin with me, let this be the moment now. With every step I take, let this be my solemn vow. To take each moment and live each moment in peace eternally; let there be peace on earth and let it begin with me."

When we can see beyond what appears to be evil, all of the golden grains of Good, we will love each other truly, for then, we will be better understood.

SPIRITUALITY, THE GOLDEN SUBSTANCE OF PEACE

Pride, ego and ignorance are incestuous and mutually beget each other. Each of these feed off the others. Such is the state of humanhood, the hypnotic state of humanity.

The hypnotic influence is rampant throughout society, disguised as authority figures of many kinds. Many people will tell you in a New York minute, "this is how I was raised," as if to say that is a proper standard by which to live their life experiences, and anyone else who is open to be influenced by them. Culture and tradition are the banners under which the hypnotic deceptions operate; thus, perpetuating their illusions of power.

A spiritual awakening to one's True Identity would undermine those with pseudo-power in the educational, political, religious, scientific and financial world. As one's consciousness rises to spiritual awareness, the error of hypnotic influence will diminish accordingly. "If *I* be lifted up," consciousness will restore peace unto your world.

To overcome the hypnotic sense of separation from our source, God, is to be as the biblical prodigal son in returning to the father's house of knowledge of self; the I Am presence that is always available for solace and peace. This place of peace can be accessed by prayer, a quieting of the mind from thoughts. True prayer is not talking to God, but being mentally still of thinking in order to *listen* to God, the voice within your own being, consciousness. Meditation is true prayer, a state of listening to the still, small voice within. Prayer is the opening of consciousness to our true being, I Am. I and my father, Source, is one.

Cease trying to influence God; it cannot be done. Can you influence mathematics, or gravity? No, but you can understand and harmonize with the principle governing each of them for right results. As that country and western song tells us, "Sometimes it seems that God doesn't care, but some of God's greatest blessings are unanswered prayer." The human does not know what's best for itself, the ego. As relates to that which we call God, It is already whole and complete. We must let It into consciousness through meditation, prayer. As we learn to pray without ceasing, peace is realized, uncovered. Being aware of the unceasing activity of Grace *is* praying without ceasing.

In humanhood there is the usual attempt to influence God or ask for certain things, to change conditions or circumstances; let it be understood God is no respecter of persons, groups, race, etc. Whosoever will, let them come and abide in the grace of God which is eternally flowing.

Due to the momentum of habit, the human mind is constantly occupied by thinking thoughts which drown out the inner voice of Self. "Behold, I stand at the door and knock." "I" is divine consciousness or the Christ within. This inner self knows only peace, abundance and prosperity. It brought the embryo from conception to birth on this planet; to an infant, child, teenager, adolescent, adult and maturity. All this growth is from within, in silence. With each advancement, we "die" to the previous stage. This dying to the previous stage is our instruction to understand that life cannot die. Life was never born and can never die. Does the caterpillar die as it transforms to the butterfly?

To live spiritually is to awaken from the mass hypnosis of humanhood. An individual does not recognize that he is dreaming until he wakes up. Only then does he become aware of the illusion that he had accepted as real because of the belief in two powers, of good and evil. He had died to the understanding of spiritual oneness of the universe. This is the message given in the Garden of Eden to Adam and Eve. "The day that ye eat the fruit of the tree of the knowledge of good and evil, that day ye shall surely die." (Gen. 2:17) What do you die to? You die to the understanding there is no duality; only oneness is real, Spiritual Oneness. To awaken to this truth, one will then put total trust in God moment by moment and say to all temptation of illusion, "get thee behind me." Illusions will be shattered by the light of understanding. Only a knowing the truth can counter a false belief no matter how long a myth or illusion has been held in the belief system of an individual.

Be clear, there is not *my* truth and *your* truth. We speak not of the same idea of truth as in a court proceeding when asked "do you solemnly swear to tell the truth, the whole truth and nothing but the truth, so help you God?" They are speaking of "facts." Facts can change but the *Truth* of which we speak is the same as principles. Principle never changes, cannot be amended nor repealed. Mathematics is such a truth or principle; so is Gravity. One can utilize or harmonize with a Truth but to violate a principle, one will experience negative consequences. "Ye shall know the truth and the truth shall make you free;" free of worry, anxiety and stress of any kind that seems to withhold the experience of peace.

Spirituality is not to be misinterpreted as meaning religion. Religion is a man-made concept of spirituality. Most religions are filled with rituals and attempts to influence God. How can that which is already whole, perfect and complete be influenced by human beings? There is nothing to pray *for* since God has already given us the kingdom of God. When one prays for things or conditions to be changed, one prays amiss. All good is already within each of us, for "the kingdom of God is within." (Luke17:21)

Spirituality is beyond words and thoughts. You must rest from thinking by practicing awareness. There is power in awareness; being a beholder without making an assumption in your mind. For *that* which you are seeking with the mind, you *are*, in your True Identity. You are the peace, abundance, joy, health. All are within you *as* you. "I am *that* I am." Through spiritual discernment a realization of Reality, truth maketh you, the individual expression, free from the concerns of the outside world.

The political and religious leaders of the world could be a catalyst to assisting millions of humans to awaken to the Truth of being if they, themselves, possessed spiritual insight and understanding. To love your neighbor as yourself would dissolve any possibilities of war wherein thousands of human lives are sacrificed in the name of patriotism to a flag representing false beliefs. There is only one Self, expressed in and as many forms of materiality whose very essence is spiritual. Global unity would be realized, when leaders awaken to Truth and "be born again."

If, however, all the religious and political leaders were to magically gain spiritual illumination, it would still rest with all other individuals to awaken of their own volition, for no one can awaken from the hypnotic influence for another. Just as no one can breathe or digest food for another, so it is with spiritual illumination which opens the door to that peace that surpasses human understanding.

Peace is not reserved for select groups of people according to race or national origin, but is reserved for any individual who is willing to sacrifice the personal sense of self, the ego. Whosoever will, let him come with an attitude of gratitude and humility.

Those individuals with a pride-filled consciousness are apt to say or feel, "Oh, look at me," when spirit uses them to show the world of hypnotized humans what has not been done before. But we ought to recall that the Master Teacher said, "of myself, I can do nothing, it is the Father within me, He doeth the works." (John 5:30) Rest and relax the frown on your brow, the tension in your shoulders, or where ever it may be, and realize that your True Identity of spirit *is* the peace and joy that you seem to be missing. To become aware that one is ignorant or hypnotized in the human condition is a great step toward knowing peace.

There is no individual who is more spiritual or less spiritual than another. God is no respecter of persons. We are all spiritual beings, all of mankind. There are, of course, different degrees of awareness of this truth of oneness.

To feel bored with life or feel lonely is a testimony of ignorance of one's True Identity (ignorance is a lack of understanding). The pathway to this level of understanding is straight and narrow, and few there be who find it. As you become open and receptive to the still, small voice from within, your growth on this path is assured. Take notice that all growth takes place from within. This is truth, physically and spiritually.

There is the story of a man looking for the Museum of Science and Industry which is on the south side of the city of Chicago. He was lost on the west side of the city. He asked a service station attendant for directions. The attendant, not knowing the location himself, replied, "Sir, if I were you, I would not start from here." You see, the man *had* to start from there because that's his only beginning place, where he *now* was located. So, it is for each of us on the spiritual path; each must start from where s/he presently is on the journey to spiritual truth. For God is One, within and *as each of us, Here and Now. Wake up!*

Fran Salzman in "Facets," beautifully puts it this way: "Ever stop to ponder what keeps your body going? What makes the rain fall on the hills, and keep the grasses growing? What is inside a blooming rose that tells it what to do? And what it is that causes the petals to fall, when that growth is through? How does an acorn know for sure an oak it has to be? And once it knows, how does it get to be that tree that we see? The order of the universe is God's alone to know; the mystery of life that causes things to grow. I have much to learn admittedly; but this one thing I see, that spark of life in the rose, is that which shines in me." Those are words of praise! Thank you, Fran Salzman, for those beautiful words. The answer to all of the questions posed from Salzman's writing is the same oneness, Life, expressing itself in and as multitude of forms while maintaining its essence of one spiritual substance.

Each one of us has a spark of divinity within us, but the responsibility to fan that spark into a flame is given to the individual. We fan that spark by acknowledging it in all our ways,

49

and it will direct our path and order our steps on that path. After entering the path, each individual must stay in his/her lane.

IT IS AS IT IS

Five two-letter words have hidden in them the secret of dwelling in peace, in this human realm of temporary existence.

To bring yourself into the *Now*, repeat the awareness exercise: Right now, without moving it or looking at it, become aware of your left thumb (pause). Now, you were not *thinking* of your left thumb, you were *aware* of it. Thoughts cease when there is simple awareness. To continue this exercise, become aware of each of the other nine fingers, one at a time. Become aware of some form across the room as you stare at it.

Do you notice the peace that ensues by simple awareness? Awareness of each breath can be the beginning of silencing the mind of incessant chatter, leading to the gateway of meditation or prayer, a listening from within. Thinking and awareness both use the human mind but, beyond words and thoughts, is *is*. The word *is* represents *Now,* or what exists at this moment, not in the past nor the future.

To be at peace regardless of the circumstance, condition, or what you observe by seeing or hearing, simply become aware of the *is-ness* of the moment without judgment. This is the secret to getting off the roller coaster of highs and lows of emotional variations.

There was this young man who was required by the court system to attend "anger management" classes. The young man even had clashes with the counselors as he attended the classes. After we introduced the awareness exercises, the youngster learned to avoid the experience of anger.

Consequently, we call it "anger avoidance" instead of anger management. It is very challenging to manage anger when you are caught up in that emotional firestorm of resentment.

The *awareness exercise* will help in "anger avoidance." One will learn to become aware of the energy of resentment before it can culminate into the emotion of anger that, too often, leads to violence.

After one passes judgment on a person or situation, there often follows a negative feeling of resentment. This inner resentment can be dissolved in its early stages, by standing aside, so to speak, and observing that energy of resentment through awareness in the same manner you were aware of your finger in the earlier exercise. Simply observe and silently repeat to yourself that the experience you are having simply "is as it is."

Be alert that you do not allow the momentum of habit to rule by commenting in your mind based on the judgment that you have made. Comments to yourself such as "that's not right," "that's crazy," "he's disrespecting me," "I'm sick and tired of him," etc. Do not write a story in your mind about what you are observing! Remember to embrace "it is as it is," "she said what she said," "he did what he did," etc. Avoid *MSU* (Making Stuff Up) in the mind.

Any reaction to what you see or hear is due to the hypnosis of humanhood. The ego sets that standard of perfection and, when it believes someone has violated that standard, it judges and reacts to the thoughts entertained in passing judgment. So in reality, you are resenting and reacting to your own thoughts. But if there is only awareness of "it is as it is" there are no thoughts that cause reaction.

Remember "the moving finger writes and having writ moves on, all of your piety or wit will not lure it back, to cancel half a line, nor all your tears wash out one word of it." "It is as it is," without comment or judgment. This may not be easy in the beginning because of the momentum of habit of "you know what they say!" "They" who?? The unawakened accept the equally un-awakened opinion of others.

I encourage you to not just "try it" but make a decision to avoid the anger emotion by practicing awareness of *Now!* Yesterday ended last night. Stay in the *now* moment of *is*: "Ye shall know the truth and the truth shall make you free" of passing judgment on other persons or situations.

We all do the best we understand at the level of consciousness and state of mind we're in. If the thief could find a reason in his mind not to take from others what does not belong to him, he would not steal. Since everyone is doing their best at the level of consciousness, why judge?

As you awaken to your True Identity of being, then know and understand that another person is not separate and apart from all that you are. Spirit is the substance or essence of all that exists regardless of the appearance. "Judge not from appearance." Forgive yourself for having judged another as being other than a spiritual being.

Any apparent problem that seems to be keeping you from that place of peace is simply a temptation that is to be rejected. If one believes in the concepts of good and evil, then the so-called problem, appearance, will continue to exist and grow.

A person with a high level of consciousness, however, is able to look through to "truth of being" and is able to drop the problem. It is seen as a problem only in your mind. As Einstein allegedly said, "you cannot solve a problem at the level of the problem." In other words, if the problem is in your mind, how then are you to use that same mind to solve the problem? It cannot be done. That would be akin to lifting your body off the floor by pulling your own boot straps. In order to drop the problem, one must first realize that the problem is appearing to be outside of you; but to accept the problem into your mind as real and a power to be overcome, fortifies a belief in two powers, good and evil.

Again, this is an all-spiritual universe, so that temptation which is appearing as a problem is founded in "as a man thinketh in his heart, so is he." (Prov. 23:7) Believing in two powers is why the mind sees the experience as a problem. As in driving an automobile, the driver looks *through* the windshield and not *at* the windshield, one must look through the problem to the truth of being that this is an all-spiritual universe. In this light of understanding, one sees clearly. Take care not to seek the advice or opinion of others concerning a problem who are equally in the dark jailhouse of ignorance of their True Identity and yours.

To remain in a peaceful state by being aware that "it is as it is," the so-called problem dissolves into its native nothingness from which it appears to have risen. By not realizing the inner being, your True Self, the surface self will always go in the direction of problem after problem. Wake up! This surface self, the ego, thrives on drama or problems. If it cannot find drama, it creates drama to perpetuate its survival. It readily misrepresents what information the five senses give it in order to live.

To live out of the mind, that the senses constantly inform, blocks that instrument (mind) from being used most effectively. The most effective use of the mind is to allow it to be a transparency for the inner being or inner light. To repeat, the sunlight does not come *from* the clear transparent window pane, it comes *through* it. But, if there is mud on the pane, the sunlight is blocked and cannot come through. If there is mud on the mind, in the form of thoughts, the inner light cannot come through to one's awareness. Then one is dependent on *inform*-ation of the five senses to endeavor to solve human problems.

Peace you cannot find, living out from the human mind. That inner self that was never born and will never die, is the source of knowing, to look to and depend on. Learn to place your focus on that inner presence that is closer than breathing, nearer than hands or feet. It is always, at peace in the eternal *Now* moment, for this is the kingdom of God.

The *inform*-ation overload that the five senses provide to the human mind leaves the individual feeling that there is more to life than what is known but unable to access it in order to experience fulfillment and peace.

Of course, the ego and pride will, by the overload of info, appear to be enriched, but these are the very same elements that keep humans from realizing peace here and now.

In reality, just as no one will ever tamper with mathematics, so no one can tamper with peace. Both can be understood and experienced but, as with all principles, they cannot be altered, amended or repealed. Learn to still the mind of incessant thinking and information to experience peace.

You will be kept in perfect peace as you focus on that which is the Source and substance of your True Identity; a spiritual being and not a human material being who, out of the momentum of habit, often mixes observation by the senses with emotions and judgment of good and evil.

The judgment of good and evil arises out of the belief in good and evil, two powers. In truth, there is omnipotence. The temptations do appear real; that is why an individual must know the truth of being that this is an all-spiritual universe. Resting in the acknowledgement that the appearance "is as it is" without judgment and emotional reaction maintains peace within your own consciousness.

If there is something to be done to change a situation or condition, get busy. That may be the reason it comes to your attention. If, however, there is nothing you personally can do, then, without judgment or emotion, simply acknowledge "it is as it is" in appearance.

THE PATH TO PEACE

The straight and narrow path to the peace place must be traveled alone, knowing that you are in reality never alone. It is only that the awakening process is an individual activity. In truth, the place wherein you presently stand is holy ground, for God is all there is. The human mind has been trained, since birth into this physical plane of existence, to see itself as separate and apart from all else. The pattern has been to solve never-ending problems of one type or another, to improve or change it. Those are distractions along the path, only concepts.

To silence the mind of the habitual pattern of entertaining thoughts, one must practice being aware of the present moment of Now. Remember the image of the plus sign (+) or the cross (✝)? The vertical aspect (|) represents *here* and *now*. The horizontal aspect or line (–) represents time, as in past, present and future. We must shatter the myth of linearity and know that time is an illusion. Every moment of existence is and has always been *Now*.

One cannot breathe for five minutes yet to come or past. You breathe *Now*. Every breath you take is *Now*. The ego, that dwells in the human mind, abhors the *now* moment because it feeds off of playing old tapes of the past in memory or being anxious about the future. The past only exists in memory; that is what keeps it alive. There are those individuals who become upset or prideful over events experienced years ago as if they are facts now. For that person it is happening *now*, with the same emotional feeling as before. Today is yesterday's tomorrow, and every instant between has been *Now*. Time is an illusion, a human construct.

One of the leading causes of anxiety about the future is the fear of death to this physical body. Life cannot die. Yes, everything that has form is temporary. That tree outside your window, one day will not be there. So it is with the ant, elephant, tiger, etc.; all are temporary; but that which is expressing itself *as* these forms, is eternal. Spirit, Life, God was never born, can never die.

Yes, we do become attracted and attached to form and, when that form is lost or exits through what we humans call death, there is often much sadness and grief. One sure way to diminish or dissolve these emotional, mental states of mind is to take an extra dosage of gratitude. A pathway laden with an attitude of gratitude leads to joy and peace. Sadness cannot survive in a grateful heart, just as darkness cannot survive in the presence of light. Be grateful for having had the experience of that loved one and know that that spirit of them yet lives. Know well that being a friend is reward of itself; simply continue to express love.

The only solution to the problems that seem to displace peace and fulfillment is to awaken to your inner Self. This Self is within your own being. The word *within* does not mean inside of your body. Just as water may be *inside* the paper cup, but paper is *within* the container or cup. The cup and paper *is* One. Remember the Master Teacher said, "I and my father are one." He also said, "the Kingdom of God is *within* you." In recognition of your True Identity you, too, will know and understand that you are one with your Source, Spirit, the Father of all, for again, this is an all-spiritual universe. "Call no man on earth your father." (Matthew 23:9)

Many human beings seem to be obsessed with finding happiness. This mystical state called happiness is temporary and fleeting. It is dependent upon sensory input to the mind. The senses constantly give or inform the mind of what appears to be *hap*-pening in the outside world. These *hap*-penings change in a *hap*-hazard fashion. If the mind interprets the *inform*-ation as good, then you feel happy. If the *inform*-ation is unsatisfactory, then unhappiness ensues. Up and down, off and on, happy and unhappy. *Happ*iness, then, is an outside job while joy comes from *within* the individual.

As stated earlier, the expressway to joy is gratitude. It is never what appears to be lost that matters, but what one has left that counts; and one always has the Source of all good at hand, closer than breathing. Your individual assignment is to become aware, know and understand that peace is always with you, but only needs to be uncovered by awakening from the mass hypnosis of humanhood. To realize the awakening, practice stillness of the mind of words and thoughts. Beyond words and thoughts is that place of peace that is within you.

As you become more and more aware of your at-one-ment with all creation, you will recognize there are no big "I's" and little "you's" except in the belief system that has been established under hypnosis.

Be open and receptive to words of truth. Often the spirit that writes words or brings new thoughts and ideas, is much more of your family of like spirits, than your own flesh and blood by physical birth. Become as a little child and learn to listen from within in lieu of what the "authorities" of the world would have you believe.

The human intellect is often loaded with knowledge of "this world" after having gone through the academic programs of colleges and universities. Be clear, however, there are no chairs of wisdom in anybody's college or university. If an individual has not gone to God in addition to having gained high degrees in formal education, one is likely to come out of such training being a sophisticated ignoramus with glimpses of peace every now and then. Being highly formally educated does not of itself prevent one from awakening to his or her True Identity; but often a belief system becomes concretized causing simple truths, that would make one free of fear in its multitude of forms, to not be recognized. John Brown Watson, the first President of my alma mater, AM&N College, Pine Bluff, Arkansas said it well: "The end of education is to know God and the laws and purposes of His universe, and to reconcile one's life with these laws. The first aim of a good college is not to teach books, but the meaning and purpose of life. Hard study and the learning of books are only a means to this end. We develop power and courage and determination and we go out to achieve Truth, Wisdom, and Justice. If we do not come to this, the cost of schooling is wasted."

These people, not experiencing peace, often look for causes outside themselves to bring that missing peace. Many such individuals professionalize being a victim of circumstances, racism etc., always playing the "somebody did me wrong" song. To know one's God-self, the Christ within, is the solution to the physical and mental apparent limitations. Beyond the horizon of human understanding is the source of infinite solitude, joy, peace and abundance. Beyond the human intellect to the "Source of being" is peace in stillness. Just as beyond the appearance of the railroad tracks coming together as one in the distance, or the sky resting on the mountain top, so it is with the illusion of knowledge that is of the intellect alone; it is limited without the understanding of the truth of oneness.

The ego, which is a false sense of self, craves knowledge for it provides for a pride-filled existence. Filling the mind with human knowledge may obscure the path to peace, for that mind cannot be opened to receive impartation from the source of all truth, God. At times, this impartation from within may be as an audible voice and you may look around for "who said that?" At other times a thought or idea simply occupies your mind that you did not put there. Where else do new inventions and discoveries come from except this infinite source of Supply?

The challenge for an individual is to step out from the conditioning and programming received from the authority figures of the world that has been thrust upon one since birth on this plane of existence. Begin to realize and know that there are no evil powers external to the human mind. Learn to see through the appearances. "Judge not from appearances" but have righteous judgement, which means to know and understand this is an all-spiritual universe with no external discords to keep you out of peace. Insight is necessary to see through the appearances of human sight. How does one acquire insight? This is achieved only by stillness of the mind of thinking thoughts. This is true prayer.

Again, prayer is not *talking* to God, but *listening* to God. What can mere humans tell an omni, all-knowing being; which God is? Rise in consciousness to know God aright!

Rest, relax in the peace of divine mind which is our True Identity now and throughout eternity, for life does not end at the grave. "I" will be with you always. Be at peace this now moment. Be content with that which *is*. The *is-ness* of now is as footprints in the sand of time, reflecting a previous state of consciousness. Be still. Be at peace. Peace, Be Still!

ONENESS

The first four words in the Bible are sufficient for a life of peace. "In the beginning God." Ponder these words. Since only God was the beginning, then it would naturally follow that *everything,* visible and invisible, would be of the same substance, God, or spirit, since God is spirit. Every human individual ought to become aware of this unity of oneness, regardless of appearances. This is an all-spiritual universe.

The Master Teacher, Jesus, knew the truth of His being in telling us that "I and the Father are one."

Your and my True Identity are one with the Father also. This is the truth of being for all form and experience. The human habit of filtering thoughts through a belief system has kept the material existence appearing real, and reacting to those appearances is deeply ingrained in the human psyche. These emotional reactions cover and block the peace that is always closer than breathing. God, Spirit, is expressed as me and you while never changing its true nature of being spiritual substance. This substance within me is identified as "I." Behold, "I" stand at the door of my consciousness and knock. This explains that feeling of not being fulfilled, the absence of being in joy and peace.

In humanhood there exist many avenues of search for this fulfillment. Words are inadequate to describe the experience of this fulfillment. The drug addict, alcoholic, food addict, sex addict, religious fanatic are all searching for the same thing, fulfillment. They are searching outside of themselves, but what they are searching *for* is *within,* not without. The kingdom or substance of God is within themselves. The word "within" does not refer to inside of one's body, but to that of which an individual is composed, the very essence or constitution of self and body; that mysterious "something" that causes things to grow from within.

Becoming consciously aware of the Source of all things, visible and invisible, activates it to appear as whatever is needed for the individual's life experience. Things needed may appear to come *through* many channels, but the things are coming *from* the one Source. Acknowledge that Source in all your ways and it will direct your goings and comings.

Imagine a flower garden; many colors, fragrances, shapes, etc., all expressing one essence, Life. There is one life, not my life, your life etc.; those are human concepts, a belief in separation. Love your neighbor as yourself, we are told. In truth there is one self, one life. As stated before, this source and substance is our beginning and remains within us eternally. "I" will never leave you nor forsake you. No human being knows how to make a sperm or egg. The one spiritual source is the origin of these cells. We come *through* our earthly parents but not *from* them. As biblical writings tell us, "Call no man on earth your father, one is your Father," God! (Matt. 23:9)

There are those individuals who believe if they were to physically move to another city, they would be more at peace. I personally felt that way as a young man, moving from city to city, to the military, back to college, etc. I one day awakened to the truth that it was not *where* I was being but *who* I was being. I came to the realization that this plot of ground whereon I stand is holy ground.

Where ever I went, I took the state of consciousness with me. So I say to you, allow a transformation of consciousness to take place right where you are, in the here and now.

Can you separate sweetness from sugar or wetness from water? Of course not, for the sameness or oneness is inherent in each one's existence. So it is with your existence with God. Spirit, God is the very existence of each of us and all other forms in the universe. The human belief of an existence separate and apart from God is as a leaf separated from the tree. While yet attached, the leaf, branch and tree is oneness in existence. To awaken to the True Identity of Self there is only peace, oneness. Though others around you may continue in a hypnotic state of humanhood, you will know the truth that makes you free from fear, lack, disease *(dis-ease)* and a host of other maladies of those who remain hypnotized. In order to wake up from the dream, one must, as Waldo Emerson said, "Get your bloated nothingness out of the way." This refers to your surface self, the ego, which is full of pride and arrogance.

The invitation is to keep your focus and awareness *on* the inner presence and *off* "this world" of form and experience. The

Master Teacher, Jesus, encouraged us to seek first the kingdom (substance) and all *things* will be added that are necessary.

To keep your mind and thoughts on "this world" of form and experience (sowing to the flesh) equates with living in the past, for form and experience are the out-picturing of a previous state of consciousness. A transformation of consciousness brings on new forms and experiences by an activity of grace; as within so without.

As the 127th Psalm tells us, "...unless the Lord builds the house, they labor in vain that build." The Lord, of course, is your very own consciousness. The principle of oneness within is as exacting as the principle of mathematics. No matter how and unknowingly an individual may pray to God for two times two to become five, or any other number except four, he prays amiss. Principles cannot be amended, altered or repealed; they can only be harmonized with by usage.

In a similar sense, peace can only be uncovered by the mind and thoughts becoming still and silent in contemplation of your inner God self, the Christ of your being. Be clear, nothing has ever happened negatively to you, nor has anyone done anything to you. It is only your acceptance of the negative situation as belonging to you, in your own consciousness. We must remember and know that God gave us dominion over everything. It is only when you forsake that dominion, the ability to dominate, that one becomes a victim in his own mind. By accepting the situation, condition or behavior of another as belonging to you, and resenting it, is what displaces *peace of mind*. The key is to stop accepting in your mind the situation, behavior or condition as belonging to you. Remember, "It is as it is." Without comment or writing a story in your mind, you have dominion to accept or not accept.

Merely because something is "a tradition" in "this world" does not necessitate you to accept it in your mind as being true or right for you. One thing that comes to mind is recognizing all of the "special" days that cause many people to become resentful, depressed or angry if they miss out on how "it's supposed to be" based on tradition. Remember some humans, at some earlier time, came up with a name for these annual "special days" or holidays. Come to know and understand that every day is made "special" by the maker of days, God.

Know, also, that the weather is always perfect weather, for this remains a spiritual universe, and spirit is always perfect. The weather does what it is assigned to do by Spirit, God. My only problem is doing what I am assigned to do by listening to the still, small voice from within. So fret not about weather conditions and changes, for that only robs you of peace.

When a branch is separated from the tree, it begins to wither and die. So it is when humans have a false sense of being separated from its source, which is God, Spirit. All so-called problems of humanity arise out of this belief of separation. This belief shows forth as a belief in good and evil, instead of dwelling in the awareness and understanding of oneness of the universe.

The temptation is in the mind, the carnal mind as Paul called it in the Bible. This mind has humanhood believing in two powers. This belief system *(BS)* is ancient from the time that Spirit warned Adam and Eve that "the day that ye eat of the tree of knowledge of good and evil, that day ye shall surely die." (Genesis 2:17) What shall you die to? To the understanding of oneness. There is no duality of good and evil powers. God, Spirit, is omnipotent.

Within each of us is the insight to see or understand the illusions of appearances. "Judge not according to the appearance." (John 7:24) The five senses are wonderful gifts, but are limited in perceiving Reality, spiritual substance. This is why it is necessary to still the mind from receiving so much information from the senses throughout the day. This stilling of the mind is the gateway to meditation, true prayer of listening to the Christ within. For one cannot seek God in the realm of thought or thinking with the human mind. Silence is key to that peace beyond human understanding, but yet is closer than breathing.

As the truth or principle of oneness takes root in consciousness of individuals the ripple effect goes out to other seekers who touch the hem of your garment (consciousness). This is the only process wherein the problems of "this world" will be solved and dissolved.

The principle of oneness of the universe is an individual's salvation when understood. In the admonition to love your neighbor as yourself is hidden the truth of there is only *(one-ly)* one self. Life itself is one. In truth there is no such thing as "my life" or "your life." There is only *one* life and it is eternal; never being born and never dying. Life is God.

Yes, the personal sense of self is a lower realm of understanding known as humanhood. This sense confirms a certain birthday, name and appearance but let me encourage you to become aware of the higher realm of Self by crucifying the lower level. That lower personal sense of self seems hard to die. This is the reason for Paul to declare, "I die daily." (1 Cor. 15:31)

Just as light dissolves darkness, so will awareness and understanding sacrifice the personal or lower sense of self with all of the problems of "this world." You will then be *in* the world but not *of* the world. This state of conscious being activates Divine Grace and the signs will follow in your life experience as peace, harmony, health, and prosperity in its many forms, including money and relationships.

Our individual assignment is to acknowledge oneness of being. If anything is done *one* time, anywhere in the world, according to or in harmony with a principle, that result or effect is available to the world. God is no respecter of persons. Principles are no respecter of persons. There is not *your* mathematics and *my* mathematics. Mathematics *is* one. The levels of understanding do vary according to knowledge and awareness.

All of us have always been one with our Source. There is no separation, only a false sense of separation, due to the mass hypnosis of humanity that perpetuates this belief. To attain conscious oneness with our Source, one must travel a spiritual path without religious indoctrination or any other human influence that distorts Truth.

The common fears of humanity can only be resolved by knowing the truth of oneness, beyond that which is visible in limited form, to the unlimited invisible presence within each being, the Source.

Hold off of believing anything for a while and have faith in your Source of being. Certainly It knows you clearly better than any human authority figure who has opinions to visit upon you, which may become another formula for confusion and a sense of separation from God, your Source. This self-centered activity of "authority figures" is separative and usually leads to conflict of one kind or another.

We always fear that which we do not understand; the fear of both psychological and physical death, the coming to an end of that which is known is *the* major fear. The thought of losing *that* disturbs the mind and absents peace.

Faith in divine Omniscience is security, for there is nothing visible nor invisible that is beyond its awareness. The long and short of it is there is nothing to fear, and that includes fear itself. Uncover the missing peace that lies serenely within you by stilling the mind to listen to the voice within.

Instead of speaking the word, as some do, listen to the word being imparted from within your own being, in silence of thinking thoughts.

The secret of life is no longer a secret; I now know that God is my life. God is all life, for life is one, expressed as infinite variety of forms and experiences. The signs of good follow this recognition of Truth. We are told, "ye shall know the truth and the truth shall make you free" of anything unlike itself. Awakening to my True Identity, I no longer pray to a God in heaven somewhere, for I am fulfilled in knowing my oneness with life, God.

The human mind cannot fathom the activity of spirit. It can be a beholder, observer of the effects of this infinite activity with an attitude of awe and gratitude. Although the human mind is made by God, it can only intellectualize *about* its creator; it can never know God.

To know God aright, a human is required to be still and silent of thinking thoughts. The awareness of the inner Christ appears when you "think not." Again, the intellect covers that inner contact which can only be made individually. No one can do it for another. Just as with breathing or digesting food eaten, no one but the individual is in charge.

To be successful in making contact with the "True Identity" of a person s/he must take his mind off the things, situations or conditions of "this world" of forms and experiences and focus on the inner being. "Seek ye first" that inner realm and things will appear as needed.

The sun of man, the inner light, will dissolve the hypnosis of humanhood when you think not; stop thinking so much and let spirit lead by impartation to and through that same mind that is now free of thinking and entertaining thoughts that are all based upon past experiences.

You will be a peacemaker on earth by entering into this state of true prayer by listening to God, the Inner Being, who forever knocks at the door of conscious awareness of every individual. Only the individual can open the door of peace and serenity through silence of the mind. "Blessed are the peacemakers for they shall be called the children of God." (Matthew 5:9) Now they hear the voice of the Father in silence of thoughts.

Out of ignorance of Truth, wars of armed conflict have been fought and thousands of humans are sacrificed, for what? The infinity of supply is sufficient for all of God's creation. Leaders, so called, of the various countries of the world apparently are only aware of the physical or material sense of existence. Some are aware of the mental realm of thinking, memory and reasoning, but the need is an awareness that the Source of all physical being and mental activity is spiritual. The knowing and understanding of this truth reveal the foolishness of war. We are one. This is a spiritual universe. So, become a peacemaker within your own being. No matter the condition, circumstance or situation, uncover the peace that is within you now. "I will be with you always, even until the end of the world," of humanhood's hypnotic influence.

You can allow the atmosphere of peace to enfold you simply by stillness of the mind from entertaining thoughts, thereby truly experiencing God. "Be still and know I Am, God." Be still and know God, I Am; for my True Identity is one with my source, God.

Just as an ice cube floating in a stream of water, the form is different but H_2O is the substance of each, the ice, solid and the liquid, water. If the ice cube could speak could it say, in fact, "I and my father is one?" "I" am not my body. The body is an instrument of "I," my God self. My True Identity, "I," has the same relationship to God as the ice cube has to the stream of water. This is true of each and every one of us. To become aware, know and understand this relationship to our creator is to dwell in that secret place of peace, tranquility and joy while experiencing heaven on earth. This relationship of oneness has always existed and shall continue to exist throughout eternity.

Humans have developed the habit of relying mainly on the five senses of seeing, hearing, tasting, touching and smelling to reaffirm their individual existence as separate and apart from each other. Beyond the horizon of each of these faculties lies the truth of being that must be spiritually discerned in silence.

Whatever activity one is engaged in lends itself to the knowing of this truth of being at any time and all the time. Just as gravity or mathematics is forever on the job, so is the principle of oneness eternally on the job, so to speak. The ice cube is at peace in the stream of water. We, too, must relax and be at peace in our oneness with God, our creator.

The invitation to awaken to your True Identity is extended by the "I" of your being. "Behold 'I' stand at the door and knock..." (Rev. 3:20) The challenge may not be simple to accept because of all the education and information that has been received since birth into humanhood, but it shall be done in this lifetime or another. As one man put it, "I have a pretty good education and it took me years to overcome it."

The invitation to discover *(dis*-cover, un-cover) the missing peace, eternally remains for every individual. You shall then have become a peacemaker, a child of God. One who remains wholly a human being is not a child of God, not having had the God experience.

It has been said that "wisdom comes with age" in the human scene, but oft times age comes alone.

There are many communities that appear to be in disarray due to violence that citizens of that community perpetuate among each other. There is talk about how to bring peace to that place, the community. Peace can only be allowed to show forth itself when there exist points of light in a growing number of individuals who are at peace within themselves. You, the reader, can be a light for others as you release the past, relax the tension in your neck and shoulder area as well as on your brow, between the eyes. You experience this release and relaxation by learning to live in the eternal *Now* moment of awareness. Be the light that shines in darkness of ignorance. The word *ignorance* is derived from the word *ignore*. To ignore wisdom and truth is to facilitate the violence and discord.

Where will wisdom be found? Where is the place of understanding? Acquaint yourself with God and be at peace. Be still in your mind and listen from within.

"Let there be peace on earth, and let it begin with me...."

THE WOMB OF SILENCE

In the search for the missing peace of humanhood there are many traditions that have arisen which add to the fog that hides the Truth from the masses. The word "belief" covers the maze of tradition that misleads the masses in their thinking process. A realization of Truth, God, comes when you "think not," when the mind is silent without thoughts of any kind. Surrender the personal sense of self.

The so-called problems of the world of humanhood clog the mind from being open and free to receive importation from within the silence of one's own being: of all so-called problems that humans experience is an intangible feeling of incompleteness or unfulfillment. The individual may feel full of religious indoctrination, artificial stimulants, food, and entertainment of various kinds but yet be unfulfilled. What s/he is absent of is being bathed in the Light of Spiritual Truth, which cannot be attained, realized by the intellect alone. It must be spiritually discerned beyond words and thoughts.

We have in our world endless testimony of power and intelligence of Silence. Ponder the trees and the unique individuality of each leaf as is the uniqueness of every human fingerprint. All trees, natural resources and sands of the sea, appeared out of Silence. In the Silence, the activity of Amazing Grace, that the human mind cannot fathom, brings forth the infinite variety of forms from the invisible to the visible.

Why worry about what you will eat, or wear? Seek first that kingdom of Silence, and the "things" will appear as needed. The peace that surpasses human understanding abides in the Silence.

To silence human thought is to enter into the Womb of Silence, to uncover the missing peace and rest from human thinking. All human thought arises out of the false belief in two powers, good and evil, whereas in Truth there is one power which is omnipotent, omnipresent and omniscient, God the Silent One.

66

Each of us has come into bodily expression from the invisible realm of existence to our present size and weight, all in silence from within. This is true of all life forms, both plant and animal throughout the world.

All human conflict would cease in the realization of this secret place of silence. The political leaders of nations on earth would show, by example, the citizens of their respective countries the alchemy of this silence. Then, there would be no possibility of wars and armed conflict. Peace on earth and good will toward man would become a growing reality. The pride of "me, myself, and mine" is dissolved in the Light of the Womb of Silence.

The outer activity in which an individual person is engaged would continue but with greater joy and gratitude in dwelling in the secret place of Silence by practicing living in the *NOW* moment of awareness.

Ideas shall flow into the mind. Ideas of expansion, growth, abundance and creativity as it becomes void of human thought. From the Source of all creation these ideas emerge. Any amount of words used concerning the intangible Silence remain just words until they are accepted into a fertile ground or consciousness; then the ripple effect will spread throughout the world community. "Let the silence begin with me," say to yourself.

Peace, Truth, is simple but it is not to be grasped with the intellect. Truth is so simple that a "Bozo" will get it and an Einstein intellect will miss it. It has nothing to do with academic achievement, which sometimes becomes a barrier due to puffed-up pride that often accompanies such achievement. This is not to imply that the Kingdom of Peace is reserved for the uneducated. Whosoever will, let him or her come to the throne of grace and understanding in silence.

Life was never born nor will ever die, for It is eternal. We humans are offered constant instructions by Life that will lead and direct us through the life experiences in this three-dimensional parenthesis of Life expressing Itself.

What we call birth, the beginning into this existence, is the ending or death to a pre-existence, of which we have no memory. The seasons instruct us of the nature of appearances. The brush, bushes, trees and weather show the temporary nature of appearances. The trees, for example, seem to die of all the leaves and fruit at the ending of a season, but Life still exists within that which we call Tree, to show forth its abundance again and again. Life cannot die or end, for Life Itself is God.

You can never find God in any material form: trees, man or book. That which we call God, Allah, Jehovah, Yahweh (all refer to the same Entity) is to be found within your own being, your own consciousness. The name by which this spiritual entity is called depends upon the tradition in which an individual was born and raised. There should never be a prejudice against another person based upon being born and raised in a tradition or belief system that is different from our own, for this is a cause for much of the conflict in the human experience. Ignorance of this simple Truth hides the peace that naturally exists within all people.

DEMONSTRATE LEADERSHIP IN ACTION

This non-judgment and non-prejudging (prejudice) naturally includes race, color, religion, nationality, gender and belief systems held by others. It is a fact that "birds of a feather flock together" because of common interests shared with others. This is not prejudice, however, but the natural unfolding of conscious events and interests of a group of two or more individuals.

A point of interest or focus could be to learn and understand more facts concerning those individuals who appear to be "unlike me." For in a flower garden there are various colors, fragrances, shapes and names of the many forms, but they all grow from the same soil, rain and sunshine. They all are expressing Life, the One Source for the existence of all the flowers. In a similar sense, the diversity of appearance of humans ought to be celebrated instead of being a cause of conflict or prejudice as is exhibited by the ignorant. "For behold, I create new heavens and a new earth: and the former things shall not be remembered, nor come to mind." (Isaiah 65:17)

There is far more to your existence than body and mind, both of which have limitations. Get acquainted with the unlimited, infinite aspect of Self through meditation, stilling the mind. Acquaint thyself with God, Life, and be at peace. ("Acquaint now thyself with him, and be at peace..." – Job 22:21)

GROUP DYNAMICS

The adage that says, "To go fast, go alone; to go far, go together," is a wise saying for those individuals who desire to experience a fuller life experience of joy and achievement. I may benefit from an idea that comes through you; to add unto that idea or by modifying it slightly, you may benefit from an idea from me, and thereby the entire group grows or benefits.

This holds true wherever there are two or more people endeavoring to work together for a common goal or purpose, whether it be a business, family, church, community, or nation.

There are certain guidelines that must be followed for a group endeavor to be successful. Paramount among these is for the personal sense of self – the ego, that personal sense that is so conscious of the labels "me, myself and mine," that self that judges and is quick to react when things do not seem to be going "my way (Be reasonable; do it my way)" – to be still and quiet.

There is the necessity to implement the "3 C's" of Communication, Cooperation and Coordination" for a successful endeavor of two or more people in any cause.

Unless you and I communicate effectively, there can be no cooperation; unless there is cooperation, there is nothing to coordinate. Hence, a successful endeavor remains a pipe dream, unrealized with pretense.

Episodes of a lack of working together for a common good are very prevalent in communities where unemployment, crime and violence remain at a high level. Playing the "victim" role is common in such communities. Communication is hardly possible if one or more of the individual participants has a prejudice or pre-established idea concerning the topic to be discussed. He "hears" another individual's point of view, but he hears it through the screen of what he thinks he already knows. Although he *hears* them, he is unable to *listen*.

"The single biggest problem in communication is the illusion it has taken place." — George Bernard Shaw

The ability to listen is an essential part of effective communication. If I am thinking about what I'm going to say while you are yet speaking, I am not listening. To interrupt you or talk over you is a habit many community residents nourish. In such communities, the personal sense of self, the ego, is very strong among the individuals, although they complain about the high rate of unemployment, crime and violence that surround them.

To awaken to one's True Identity, breathing or digesting food are a few of the things that must be done alone. To work alone is also necessary on occasion, but to operate alone where there ought to be group co-operators, people working together, the personal sense of self must be sacrificed in order not to be so easily offended by the words and actions of others in the group.

Everyone is expressing or behaving at his or her level of understanding, including you and me. Why, then, should we sit in judgment of each other's behavior? Let us assist each other by using the gift of verbal and nonverbal communication that we all may grow.

Cooperation of those individuals who are communicating within a group is essential. To repeat, "To go fast, go alone; to go far, go together" has been proven time after time in the corporate world of business, which contrasts vividly with the world of communities that have not learned how or the value of cooperative effort. A "ripple effect" of people working together for a common purpose is apparent far beyond the center of activity of a team effort.

The creation of job opportunities and being an image of inspiration for others, especially the young people of a community, are fringe benefits of people cooperating with each other.

The third of the "3 C's" in any successful endeavor where two or more people are engaged is that of *coordination* of those who are *communicating* and *cooperating*.

In order to effectively *coordinate* the activities of those individuals who are cooperating with each other, there should be a director or leader to synchronize those group activities for a successful endeavor to be realized in operating businesses in the community that will provide jobs and positive images for young people.

In Nature we see geese flying toward the south in the fall season of the year and toward the north in the spring season of the year. We never see them fly alone but are organized in a group formation. It is said that they fly higher and faster in formation, with less individual energy expended. These birds obviously did not go to school to learn the route to fly, nor how to organize in formation. They are guided by an invisible Spirit that is within all form; in rhythm with the universe.

Fortunate indeed are groups of humans working together whose director, or leader, does not depend on the human intellect alone but listens to guidance and inspiration from within in coordinating those individuals who have developed the spirit of cooperation which is the natural result of effective communication. Working together effectively is a constant challenge for those who have a strong personal sense of self, who are ego-driven with pride and arrogance.

The frustration and anger in such a community of high joblessness and violence are often attributed to external factors while not realizing the situation has evolved out of a community consciousness steeped in selfishness and ignorance of utilizing the cement of the 3 C's of communication, cooperation and coordination to uncover the missing peace in the community. The acronym of team effort says it well: *T*ogether *E*ach *A*chieves *M*ore.

An automobile and the human body are excellent examples of different systems that are well-coordinated. The human body, of course, is created and coordinated by God, Spirit, Life Itself.

The principal thing that prevents people from working together for a common purpose is their personal sense of self is so strongly conditioned that it perceives that it will no longer exist if it is found out to be in error or wrong. "Me, Myself and Mine" often are pride-filled expressions of the ego or personal sense of self. The impersonal "I, Self" knows that it is simply an instrument for service of others.

One must "die daily" to that personal sense of self as the True Self is evolving. This is possible despite having been heavily conditioned by the world of humanhood's belief in good and evil.

In a group of people, communication is near-impossible if either participant participates from a preconceived idea or belief. This is why it is necessary that the personal sense of self, i.e., ego, must be parked outside the door.

Ignorance, pride, jealousy, resentment and anger are tools that the ego uses to keep people in a sense of separation, unable to work together for a common beneficial purpose. Ignorance and pride beget each other.

71

Unable to recognize these weaknesses within himself, the ego-based individual plays the blame game and sees himself as being a victim of circumstances. All human problems are of the same nature: ignorance of Truth principles that govern success.

To ignore is the root of ignorance, which is due to a lack of understanding. To inwardly confess one's ignorance is to begin to dissolve the ego, a real challenge for many or most individuals who are steeped in "tradition," a doctrine of humanhood.

Be it known that many customs and traditions are as poisoned honey, sweet and comfortable to experience, but which limits your growth or destroys you. "This is how I was raised," is hardly a standard by which Truth is to be measured and other people are to follow.

The humility of a cooperative attitude is essential for growth in any group endeavor. What is found, however, in ineffective group dynamics is over-active pride-filled ego. The ego's primary concern is "me, myself and mine," and it is ever ready to react emotionally to any disagreement or hint of criticism. The ego always wants to be "right" in its thoughts and actions, and it will defend itself forever.

With this attitude being so widespread, the effect is that others operate the businesses in the community, taking out of that community millions of dollars that no longer circulate for the benefit of residents of that community.

The businesses present in such a dysfunctional community are not to be blamed, just seizing opportunity.

YOUR WORD BECOMES YOUR WORLD

"The whole manifested world goes to show us what use we have made of the Word – Inner Speech." — Neville

Your Word, Your World: one "L" makes the difference. That "L" is Love, which is God.

You are encouraged to change your habitual negative inner self-talk and start a new positive inner dialogue that mirrors or reflects life experiences you prefer to have, that are of joy. Your Word, inner self-talk, transmutes into future facts of experience, your world.

If one's inner talking is based upon present facts of experience, then tomorrow is likely to be the same as today and yesterday. This is why some people have concretized experiences in life and say, "same old, same old," meaning nothing has changed. Inner self-talk is sowing seeds of future actions and experience; as you sow, so shall you reap. "In the beginning was the Word." (John 1:1)

Your WORD grows to be your WORLD by a means or a principle no human mind can comprehend, but the evidence of inner self-talk matching outer experience is irrefutable. As within, so without; the outer realm of form and experience reflects the inner conversations and mood of individual minds. Unless there is a transformation of consciousness, out of which self-talk (Word) grows, there will not be a change in the World of experience of the person. An individual's collection of beliefs about one's self is called his self-concept. A transformation of this belief system is necessary before more harmonious or enjoyable experiences can be realized. We say "enjoyable" because all experience, good or evil, is in harmony with the individual self-concept and his Inner Word or self-talk.

Neville writes: "Talking to oneself is a habit we all have. Most of us are totally unaware that our inner conversations are the cause of the circumstances and experiences of our lives. To attempt to change your experience before you change your inner talking is to struggle against the very nature of things. Our present mental conversations do not recede into the past like people believe, but advance into the future to confront us as invested or wasted words."

Invested words confront us with ideal experiences. Wasted words bring more of the same unchanged experiences that are not wanted or preferred.

SOWING AND REAPING

Being born and raised on a farm in the Bethlehem community of Springfield, Arkansas, I had the opportunity to observe and learn the routine of planting (sowing) various kinds of seeds, e.g., cotton, corn, peas, beans, potatoes and many others, into the soil of the family farm. Every seed knew its destiny; the cotton seed never became beans nor any other plant except cotton.

These lessons learned from my farm experience aided my understanding of life experiences that people have who are at the human low level of consciousness that we, as humans, are born into this dimension of time and space. Biblical scripture tells us that we will experience the consequences of our thoughts and actions; we reap what we sow. (Galatians 6:7-9)

My farm experience taught me that because of a Law of Increase one always reap more than one sows. Otherwise, there would be no motivation for a farmer to plant and harvest. This is the lot or condition of the human experience of life until a transformation of consciousness is allowed wherein an individual begins to live by grace. In that passage of Galatians 6:29, it is stated that to sow to the flesh is to reap corruption. The "flesh" is appearance, effect or life experiences that an individual has. To sow or focus on effects is to plant seeds (sow) for future experiences of the same nature. This is referred to as reaping corruption. In other words, life experiences do not change, as if they are concretized.

One who is in a higher state of consciousness does not deny the experience or effect but does not focus on them nor judge them as good or evil, but keeps one's focus (sowing) on the Infinite Invisible, God. This individual is sowing to the Spirit and reaping Life everlasting, living by grace and taking no thought for his life experiences. This individual is at peace with Self, and in Joy. Proverb 3:6 encourages us to acknowledge Him (The Infinite Invisible) in *all* our ways and He shall direct our path (by an activity of grace unfolding). We are encouraged to keep our mind stayed on the *I Am* of Being, regardless of life experiences. "I am *that* I am," and so are you. We are one in Truth Identity. To realize this Truth is to uncover, and to stay in, peace.

In the beginning is the Word (consciousness level) and the Word becomes flesh (effect experience). We must learn to judge not by appearance but keep our mind stayed on the Infinite Invisible Source, out of which all visible form and experience emanates; the form and experience are temporary, however.

To take thought of revenge toward another is to "sow to the flesh" and block awareness of the Now by reliving the past. The law of sowing and reaping is the same for all human beings. Romans 12:19 tells us "vengeance is mine," so drop the idea of seeking revenge. The assignment for each of us is to be at peace while being aware of the ceaseless bounty of Jehovah's grace as our sufficiency.

Awaken to the Spiritual Oneness of the Universe, showing forth as infinite variety of forms and experience; the essence, substance remains the same oneness. Spirit is the giver and the gift by an activity of grace.

Each of us is a living testimony to the power and creativity of the Infinite Invisible to express Itself as you, me, every leaf, fingerprint, all form and experience. The law of sowing and reaping is a law of justice more exacting than any law of justice that can be legislated by human assembly. The only practice that will neutralize the law of sowing and reaping in the human scene is to rise in consciousness to live by grace.

Cease giving attention to that which is not wanted; to do so is "sowing to the flesh" and to reap corruption of similar experiences in the time-based future. Reaping is always in due season. Reaping may be experienced in this parenthesis (–) or on the other side of the veil into the next parenthesis. Life is eternal, therefore experiences (reaping) in this parenthesis may have been sowed in a previous existence. Unless and until one repents from the hypnosis, ignorance of humanhood, peace and fulfillment will remain elusive.

INNER SELF TALK

- It is our inner conversations which make tomorrow's facts (experiences)
- It is possible to solve any situation by the proper use of imagination and self-talk
- Why call young *people* "kids?" The baby goat is a kid! Let us call young humans, "young man," "young woman," "young people," or "children"
- Why call yourself "sorry," using the Lord's name (I Am) in vain? "Pardon me" or "I apologize" is sufficient; *never,* "I am sorry." *Never* use a word

unlike *good* after the words "I Am," e.g., "I am broke, tired, sick, angry, lonely, etc."

- Who started saying, "bless you" when another sneezes? Why follow a foolish tradition?
- Why perpetuate a human tradition that has no value merely because, "this is how I was raised?"
- Custom and tradition keep the sex topic a "hush-hush" topic that wreaks havoc in the life experiences of millions of people, young and old. This includes, but is not limited to, incarceration in prison, abortions, and other unwanted pregnancies. Over eight billion people on earth exist due to sexual intercourse of a male and female, so why treat the subject of sex in a secretive manner?? Union of male and female is God-ordained, Principle-based!

"AS A MAN THINKETH IN HIS HEART, SO IS HE"

We can absolutely depend on the absolute justice of the law of "as within, so without." No help comes from without. Those that seem to help or hinder us are simply vehicles by which that law creates the form and experiences of our lives. The *Within-ness* is also known as *consciousness* levels.

To attempt to change My World of experiences before I have a transformation of consciousness would be an exercise in futility, and to deceive myself.

To realize a transformation, one must die daily to the personal sense of self by developing a listening attitude while the mind is silent of words and thoughts. Prayer without ceasing is a stilled mind that is emptied of the concepts and beliefs of tradition and culture of humanhood. True prayer is not talking to God, but listening to the "still, small voice" that is imparted from within, a silent, listening attitude of mind. What can humans tell mathematics, gravity, or God?

Become aware of your general mood and inner conversation and you will discover that the numbing influence of habit appears outwardly as your world by an activity of your own making. Cease playing the role of victim of other people or circumstances. Look within yourself, your consciousness, for the cause and solution of life experiences. Principle is no respecter of person, race or nation. The principles of gravity, mathematics or aeronautics are universally one and the same for all who make use of each, regardless of ethnicity. The solution to all seeming problems of the World, is not of this World, the environment of the senses. That World is a form of imprisonment. Break free from the jailhouse of ignorance, which is simply a lack of understanding. Now is the time for Present Moment Awareness (PMA).

The eternal *NOW* moment is offered to us as a stepping stone toward awakening to the Truth of Being. The hypnosis of humanhood exists only as long as it takes each individual to become aware of his or her True Identity. Your mindset at the moment may be adulterated with doubt which is part of the hypnosis, years of having accepted conclusions that have become a part of belief systems that limit the inherent potential we all received by the givingness grace of God, our Source and Substance. Remember, all human thought is based upon the hypnotic belief in two powers, good and evil. Truth reveals only One Power, which is omnipotent, omniscient and omnipresent – God.

In the beginning was the Word, and the Word manifested as the World by The Infinite Invisible power that shows forth *as* visible form and experience. The Source and Substance (the Giver and the Gift) are one – Spirit (God). The environment of the senses testifies to the inner mood and conversation of each individual, a record of the past; as within, so without.

You are never punished *for* your sins; you are punished *by* your sins. A violation (sin) of any principle brings forth the consequences of that violation, which is called "punishment." "As you sow, so shall you reap."

The paralysis of custom and tradition govern many people, if not most, by laying a railroad track on which their belief system rests or travels. An individual has the choice at any moment to awaken from the hypnotic influence of the world of humanhood; to be *in* the world but not *of* the world. This realization must come to all who awaken to their True Identity and live by the activity of Grace.

NO DIRTY WATER

In this third-dimension world of existence there appear to be infinite varieties of form: plants, animals, water, fire, etc.; things seldom are what they appear to be to the senses. Since this is an all-spiritual universe, the substance of all form is one – Spiritual.

Our concepts of the forms are endless. Whatever we call a certain form is a concept, an abstract idea to identify that thing. A chemical combination of two atoms of hydrogen and one of oxygen is called water, H_2O. The essence of that liquid called water is spiritual (remember, this is an all-spiritual universe). Nothing can alter Reality. Although sediments of various kinds may be dissolved in or mixed into the liquid called water, H_2O of itself remains the same. Spirit shows forth as water, H_2O.

To understand the truth of this statement helps us to know and understand that there is no evil person. There may appear to be dirty water or an evil person, but both points of view are hypnotic beliefs. Right where evil appears to exist to the senses is Truth. To know this in spite of appearances is the beginning of a healing for you and for the object on which the concept of evil was pinned. There is forgiveness required; first, to forgive oneself for having judged another person as evil and, second, to forgive the other individual by knowing their True Identity.

Every step toward knowing Truth that makes one free is at the expense of things and beliefs that humans hold dear and love.

The belief in duality, of good and evil, will have to die as one travels in understanding on the path toward Truth. In order for an awakening from the hypnosis of human belief in good and evil, many indoctrinating academic and theological doctrines must be shattered in the individual's belief system. Thought and behavior arise from belief systems. Change the tracks of belief, thoughts and feeling, and behavior will automatically be altered. Indoctrination is the central mechanism by which the masses are controlled. "Tell me what a man believes, and I'll tell you what he will do."

As an example of this mass manipulation, the topic of sex has become a "hush-hush" topic. Although over eight billion people on earth arrived as a result of male and female sexual intercourse, most adults learned about sex from a buddy in a kind of underground whispering campaign instead of being taught the facts about such a universally important subject.

Much divorce, separation, prison incarceration, and more are offshoots of this custom and tradition that assure ignorance by the masses, thus causing untold misery in a multitude of forms. Yet the momentum of habit, custom and tradition continues to enslave.

Why do mothers and fathers neglect to teach their male and female children what they have come to understand and make sure they receive the proper instruction on this very important subject in order that their children will not be misled down a path of many problems due to the absence of these instructions?

The sex act between males and females of all species, not just humans, is the path through which Life chooses to transform Itself into material forms. These forms are temporary, to say the least, but that which is unseen, without form, is eternal. Life is eternal. (2 Cor. 4:18)

Again, children come *through* us but not *from* us. Neither mother nor father knows how to make a liver, heart, kidney or toenail. Spirit is the Source.

The custom and tradition of emphasizing the physical, pleasurable sensation that addicts untold millions of people, male and female, would be reduced if sex were approached spiritually.

As a useful beginning, let us remove the "taboo" label from the topic of sex and move the topic to a necessary one of awareness, knowledge and understanding in order that humanity continues to grow in its conscious reconnection with its Source.

Far too many parents say to children, "I'm your mother (father), not your friend," as if an older (and supposedly wiser) parent is not to engage in dialog about certain topics, especially of a sexual nature. The havoc that many people experience later in life may be avoided when silence on the topic of sexual concerns is ended.

Abortions and other unwanted pregnancies will be reduced significantly when the spiritual aspect of sex is acknowledged, thereby elevating it beyond mere entertainment and sensationalism by many individuals who seem to be addicted to sexual activity while dwelling in ignorance of the ramifications involved, including personality disorders of children of unwanted pregnancies. This feeling of rejection is communicated to the unborn child in utero and after birth!

All feelings are a part of the unborn child's development, whether it is of love, fear, insecurities, anger or whatever, because the mother and child feast on the same mental, physical and emotional diet due to their connection of oneness during gestation. This is a reason that the father of the unborn child ought to play a significant role in assisting the mother to be happy, joyous, secure, and well-fed in all aspects. Anyone, of course, can fill this role if the father is not available.

The term "coming out of the closet" is often used in describing the sexual orientation of individuals; this would be an appropriate term to uncover the factual truths about the sex topic in general, so that future generations will cease to be trapped in the jailhouse of ignorance that has wreaked havoc in the life experience of untold millions.

To confirm the need for such awakening, ask several of your acquaintances how they learned about the sex topic; was it "hush-hush" with the adults and other "authority figures" in their lives? Are *you* embarrassed to discuss the sex topic? Why?

As one learns to still the human mind and taste the silence, peace will be realized within one's being; a sense of what's important changes.

I HAVE

"To him that has shall be given, to him that does not have shall be taken away even that he has." (Matt. 13:12)

That which is like unto itself is drawn. The more I think of what I lack or don't want, I'm right and will experience it, more want, lack.

To think *of* is to lack; to think *from* is to have. This is the Law of Assumption.

Overcome the world (that which is inward is always overcoming the outer). My inner consciousness constantly takes form and experience.

We do not see things as *they* are; we see things as *we* are. The world tends to be a mirror of individual consciousness.

THOUGHTS TO PONDER

- "Conventional rules of behavior in so-called advanced parts of the world are unnatural and contribute to Self-repression"
- Self is God; express Self, God
- All human thought is based upon the belief in two powers, good and evil. There is only One Power, God!
- IPOD of Life is the path to successful life experiences:
  - *I* *P*rioritize, *O*rganize, *D*iscipline
- When the mind becomes a clear transparency for Truth, then it no longer knows good and evil; until then it knows good and evil and can never know God, peace, or harmony of life experiences; the mind, therefore, can never know God!
- The way society punishes crime does as much to create the criminal as does temptation
- (T)Here – The good we seek (there) is right here in potential; awaiting our recognition and acceptance
- Try or Tri (mind, body, soul); cease *try*ing it and *tri* it
- Consciousness is the substance of...
- Things hoped for, evidence of things not seen (unseen). Believe more in what you don't see. (2 Cor. 4:18)
- Faith and Consciousness *is* one (Faith, Consciousness, is what I Am)
- Thoughts and feelings run on the tracks of belief

THE TOMB OF IGNORANCE

- The ego is glorified
- Pursuing Happiness is illustrated by the Prodigal Son (Luke 15:11). It's not in the land, but in the man. It's not where you are, but who you are. Allow

81

Joy from Within instead of chasing happiness without
- Peace, you cannot find, through use of the human mind; living out from the mind by the entertaining thoughts of good and evil is misusing the human mind
- You pray and receive not because you pray amiss, by multitude of words
- Any silencing of the mind brings, uncovers, reveals peace, joy and harmony, which always exist but cannot be experienced because they are blocked, covered by the multitude of concepts, beliefs of humanhood
- The *sense* of things is not Reality, only illusion

PRODIGAL SON

Poverty is a state of mind (consciousness), not a financial condition.
- The activity of the Divine Mind within me *is* the Activity of Grace.
  This is my Supply
- Degrees of growth and understanding are by Grace
- "Don't 'should' on me;" It Is As It Is

Judgment and/or impatience triggers the emotion of resentment which, if unaware, leads to anger and violence

To curb violence, deal with the roots, which are *judgment* and *impatience*
- Escape from imprisonment of the senses through revision, forgiveness
- Desire and expectancy must become one
- "We are led to believe a lie when we see *with* the eye, not *through* the eye."
  — Blake
- "When you call yourself an Indian or a Muslim or a Christian or a European, or anything else, you are being violent. Do you see why it is violent? Because you are separating yourself from the rest of

mankind. When you separate yourself by belief, by nationality, by tradition, it breeds violence. So a man who is seeking to understand violence does not belong to any country, to any religion, to any political party, or partial system; he is concerned with the total understanding of mankind." — J. Krishnamurti

Living in the *Now* will dissolve worry and anxiety for everyone who practices being grateful in this Now moment.

The non-existent future does not lend itself to harmony in any form, as *Now* is realized as eternal life. Eternal life is *Now*, eternally. Existence is always here and now. Time and space are illusions of the human mind. God (Spirit) *is* Now.

OMNIPRESENT (ALWAYS NOW), AND OMNIPRESENCE (ALWAYS HERE)

To learn to live by being aware of the Now moment requires a certain amount of discipline but the peace and joy experienced make the effort well worthwhile. In the hustle and bustle of daily living in this world of human tradition and culture, peace and joy are realized by an extreme few people, although it is readily available to everyone because it is no respecter of persons. As you gain understanding of your True Identity, beyond the personal sense of self, indeed you will become the light in a world of darkness, ignorance.

The understanding of which I speak is contrary to human beliefs, which are based upon concepts. These concepts must be surrendered. This surrender is an individual's transition within one's own consciousness.

To be aware, i.e., to know and understand that God (Spirit) is the substance of everyone's very existence, is to awaken to what is known as Christ Consciousness. This is the same state the Master Teacher Jesus implored us to seek first, and "all these things" will be added as this state of consciousness is reached.

The apparent confused state of humanhood is perpetuated because the newborn children sit at the feet of parents and other "authority figures" that have been indoctrinated, programmed and conditioned by similar "authorities" themselves. The root word in "authority" is *author*, whom we know writes scripts, except in the cases being referenced. The authorities we speak of write scripts for people's lives, or belief systems, that are not based on Truth principles; hence, the chaos observed throughout the world and many individual experiences.

As individuals begin to "dwell in that secret place of the most high" by living in the Now moment, the ripple effect will go out to heal others in their search for peace and joy. That secret place of the most high is a secret due to the fact that few individuals have uncovered it in order to reach the high state of consciousness as encouraged by the Master Teacher Jesus when he said, "If I be lifted up." *"I"* is your very own True Identity, and mine. We are One in Source and Substance; we are Spiritual Beings.

By being the Light, there can be no darkness of ignorance to be active within you. Darkness does not exist where ever and whenever light shines. The True Identity of each of us is the Light and, as each individual awakens to the Truth of being, he realizes as did the Master Teacher that, "I am the Light of the World." *"I"* is the Way, the Truth and Life.

Let it be emphasized that the personality or personal sense of "I" is not the same, because this ego-based entity believes in two powers, good *and* evil. This latter state is that of humanhood that has been programmed and conditioned by tradition and "authority figures."

Come out from among them; be in the world, but not of the world of humanhood. Know and understand that the human mind is an instrument to receive instruction and guidance from the Inner Light when it, the mind, is free of thoughts to become a clear transparency as a window pane is for sunlight.

Time is an illusion, since it is always *Now*. It makes no difference how long it takes on the path to become the Light or to awaken to the Light (that you already are in your True Identity). Never give up, never ever stop until you realize your oneness with God. There have been generations of indoctrination and programming of the belief of separation from God in humanhood's hypnosis.

The Kingdom of God is within every one of us, awaiting our awakening from the slumber of humanhood. God is no respecter of individuals; the sun shines on the so-called just and unjust. Mathematics is the same for everyone. Whosoever will, let him or her come to the fountain of Truth in the silence. Fear not, "I" am within you always.

You are not limited by your past experiences, ever. The starting point of evolving to being, having and doing is here and now. To have a new experience, let go of the concept or belief of who you are and know the Truth of being, wholly spiritual. Yesterday ended last night. Experience a new beginning of a higher level of consciousness that, by the activity of grace, will out-picture as new experiences of health, relationships, finances or whatever the need may be.

UNVEIL THE LIGHT OF TRUTH BY AWAKENING TO TRUTH IDENTITY

In talking about Truth, some people have said, "What is true for me may not be true for someone else." Yes, we do use that word "truth" loosely when talking or writing about *facts,* which change and never remain the same except in memory. The Truth of which we speak here never changes, for Truth – with a capital "T" – is synonymous with principle, spirit or God. You have heard it said that "God never changes." Principles, such as mathematics, gravity, aerodynamics, never change; they cannot be amended nor repealed.

Peace is such a principle or Truth. We cannot experience peace by willpower. Not by might, nor by power, but by my spirit. (Zech. 4:6) It unfolds from within our own conscious being by an activity of Grace, or the givingness of God. We can prepare ourselves to receive or unveil peace by quieting the mind from entertaining constant streams of thought. Not only will peace appear but also new ideas will surface, to dissolve or neutralize what appeared to be a problem in the form of disease, relationship inharmony, or lack in its multitude of forms.

To unveil or uncover can only take place when something already exists. The peace that is missing in one's life experiences is hidden from realization by the human mind, but it already exists within.

85

DIS-EASE BRINGS ABOUT DISEASE

It matters not how long the darkness of ignorance has appeared to exist, the instant the Light of Truth comes to consciousness, there is no darkness. Darkness cannot co-exist with light. Darkness is simply the absence of light. Darkness is unreal; Light is real.

Why, one may ask, is it necessary for thoughts to be still in order to experience God? All human thoughts are based upon a false belief in two powers, good and evil. Truth, or God, is the one and only power. "Ye shall know the Truth and the Truth shall make you free" of being mired in human thinking, which is the root of not being at peace.

The human mind always aspires to be something it believes is greater, better or other than what exists in this moment. The human mind always tries to improve humanhood, which causes stress and distress. Fulfillment is seemingly absent to the human mind because it is comparing and desiring that which is not quite enough. Although perfection already exists in the realization of God and is always omnipresent, the human mind, by being anchored in a belief system of materiality, is always seeking to improve conditions, circumstances and situations. To occupy the human mind with thoughts of this nature is to create enough seeds to produce a crop of feelings that could never be in harmony with peace, because peace would remain thinly veiled.

A listening attitude must be developed throughout the day and night, no matter what outer activity one may be engaged in. To continue listening from within will bring about a transition in consciousness where you will dwell in that secret place of joy and peace, no matter what the outer experiences are. They, too, will be transformed by an activity of grace. The human mind is incapable of comprehending this activity, for it is the givingness of God. The only requirement is that the mind be quiet and still in a listening attitude. Peace must be realized individually. Beneath appearances is the missing peace. Judge not by appearance. Judge righteous judgment by knowing the Truth, free of discord, inharmony, lack, worry, anxiety and all other maladies of humanhood. Do you agree that this is a worthy goal.

CONVERSATIONS FOR TRANSFORMATION

An individual walking alone down the street, talking to himself aloud, is usually thought to be strange or mentally ill. The fact that all human beings talk to themselves within their own mind is equally strange but is accepted as normal.

Most of us believe that these conversations recede into the past, not understanding that they advance themselves into the future to be out-pictured as experiences of life. We can readily see why certain types of experiences seem to be concretized. It is because the mental conversation is usually concerning what is appearing as an experience at the moment, and *seeds for future* similar experiences are being planted by the present mental conversation; sowing to the flesh, reaping corruption.

It becomes incumbent upon the individual to still the mind of incessant thinking of thoughts in order to realize Spirit as the only power for change, and not our thoughts. We are encouraged to seek first the Kingdom (or substance) of Spirit, and the experience and form will change by an activity that the human mind will never understand, for the transformation is an activity of Grace, the givingness of Spirit, God.

So the inner conversation becomes a conversation with God, without words or thoughts as we humans know them. Silence is the communication with Spirit, God. True prayer is listening to God when the mind "think not," is not thinking by entertaining a multitude of thoughts. Peace will appear in one's world of experiences.

In the world of humanhood there have been lectures, sermons, outer prayers and food fasting for ages, and yet wars, interpersonal conflicts, violence, poverty and disease have not subsided.

A fasting from mental conversations, into silence of thoughts in order to listen *for,* and *to,* that Inner Voice of peace, joy, and harmony, will show forth as abundance of all good from the invisible Source of all creation.

The momentum of habit, of the human mind entertaining thoughts, is so strong that only a few will experience the silence right early. It will take practice of awareness and meditation in order to renew the mind, so that you may be more, do more and have more joyful relationships, abundant finances, physical well-being and harmony in body, mind and spirit.

The inclination of one's belief, from which thoughts emerge, causes a transformation of the invisible to become visible proof of what is believed, even if it is error thinking, not in harmony with principle or Truth. It will appear in human experience to perpetuate humanhood hypnosis

The term, "you know what they say," is often used to influence others to a certain type of behavior that is in harmony with tradition. Who are "they?" If the tradition has no basis in Truth principle, it need not be followed just to maintain friendship with someone.

AVOID STRESS, SILENCE THE MIND

Realize that nothing external to you has any power to stress you. Learn to simply be aware, observe the person or situation as if at a distance from you, as a spectator. The event that you are experiencing is neither good nor evil; it simply *is*. A judgment of good or evil is based upon a belief held in the mind of the beholder. The personal sense of "I," "me," or "mine" is feeling threatened and the automatic feeling of resistance is activated if you are ruled by that personal sense of "I," which has no reality in Truth. A dying daily to the ego is necessary. Take your mind and thoughts off "this world" and place your entire focus on the spirit within you, that impersonal "I."

Do not accept as belonging to you whatever the temptation calls itself. This is a universe of order, although the human mind has been hypnotized to believe otherwise. "Ye shall know the truth, and the truth shall make you free" of this hypnotic influence.

If you become conscious of being sad or angry step aside, so to speak, and be aware of the emotion. Never say to yourself, "I am sad," but there appears to be sadness, separate and apart from you, your True Self, I AM.

The human mind is frightened by information that the five senses feed it that it does not understand. We always fear that which we do not understand.

One can access that inner Kingdom of peace by stilling the mind of thoughts about "this world." This quietness is prayer, for then the mind can receive the word of God, impartations from within. Pray without ceasing by realizing that quietness throughout the day, no matter what outer activity you may be engaged in. "In quietness and confidence shall be your strength." (Isaiah 30:15)

Many people are imprisoned by the mind's incessant entertaining of thoughts to the point of being unable to sleep. The mind is making so much noise playing old tapes in memory of past experiences. This can be ended as a habit by practicing living in the now moment, through being aware of each finger on both hands; or being aware of breathing. Notice that *thoughts stand still in awareness* because you come into the *Now* moment; not past or future, but *Now*.

Every breath taken in the eternal Now moment can be used, not only to bring oxygen into the body, but also as an instrument or vehicle to carry you into the presence of God. That inner presence awaits recognition within the silence and quietness of the mind. Peace will be discovered in such times when you think not. To repeat, anything that can be uncovered must already exist. Peace *does* already exist within each of us.

As Joel S. Goldsmith says, "Every human being is in prison, the prison of the mind and the body," because this is all he is aware of. He cannot understand anything that he is not aware of. He cannot, with deliberate intent, uncover the peace if he is unaware that It already exists within him. He knows about the vital organs that are *inside* of the body or the education that the mind has received, but he remains unaware (ignorant) of that which is *within*, his True Identity of I AM.

Many times, the influence of parents and other "authority figures" in the life experiences at an early age must be overcome. These "authority" people can only express at their level of consciousness. As individuals reach the age of maturity, each has the responsibility to break out of the prison of ignorance that limits them in awareness to the mind and body, and seek a higher realm of consciousness, by throwing off the influences of earlier periods of existence and "come out from among them," and be *in* the world but not *of* the world about you.

Peace you cannot find while lost in the human mind. The mind is constantly being informed with *inform*-ation by the five senses as to how things, conditions, situations or circumstances appear. St. John 7:24 encourages us to judge not according to the appearance, rather to judge righteous judgment that this is an all-spiritual universe, and the appearance is the out-picturing of states and stages of consciousness according to spiritual law. A transformation of consciousness is necessary to produce a transformation of human experience.

The mind must be taken off the appearances and focus placed on Spirit within; keep your mind stayed on God, Truth. Become choiceless, aware of the *is-ness* of the *Now* moment and allow peace to appear in your life experiences. Behold, "I" (Peace) stand at the door of your consciousness and knock.

This allowing cannot be done with the intellect (the mind) alone, but with intelligence – the heart and mind in harmony, to uncover the Missing Peace, Reality or God within you. This peace is closer than your breathing, nearer than hands or feet. It requires stillness of the mind as prayer, which is choiceless awareness of the power of *Now*, the *is-ness* of Now.

Pray without ceasing, regardless of what your outer activity may be. Enter your closet of that secret place; dwell in that secret place of a high consciousness, to experience the peace that surpasses human understanding. Yes, you will then be *in* the world but not *of* the world. It is a place of peace that only the individual can reach and experience. To go *far*, one must begin near, from here, where he presently dwells. That inner urge that is felt within one's being is God's Word or impartation letting the individual know to push forward to new heights, new ground of unfoldment.

The *is-ness* of this present moment is in harmony with Truth principles. If the human mind interprets it to be other than perfect, that assessment arises out of a lack of understanding of the perfection of God and the nature of error thinking. Since we say that God is omnipotent, all-power, where does any other power exist except as an illusion of the finite human mind that is filled with beliefs?

The error is of the belief system (BS) of the mind. Peace is hidden from the experience of the individual because of ignorance, an ignoring of Truth, God. All that the Sun *is* is expressed in every sunbeam. All that God *is* is expressed as you, me, allness. The illusion of separation must be overcome by knowing the Truth. Just as darkness disappears in the presence of light, so does ignorance disappear in the knowing of Truth.

Stop fighting and resisting errors in whatever form it presents itself, whether as relationship conflicts, apparent lack, disease or seeming loss of a loved one. We are encouraged in biblical scripture to "resist not evil." By resisting, we empower the illusion being resisted. Instead, turn within to silence the mind by practicing choiceless awareness of the *now moment*. The momentum of habit may challenge entering into this "peace place" for a while, but make a decision to enter, not merely to "try it," which is to dilute your own resolve. The ordinary human does not like to have Truth revealed by dwelling in the secret place of silence. Come out from among the ordinary man and be the unique individual that your fingerprint already testifies you to be. "'Tri'" it with mind, body and soul.

To the young people of the communities, become aware of the persuasive power of the lyrics of certain songs and how this lodges in the subconscious mind to cause one to act in other than a legitimate manner, to cause pain and suffering to yourself, family and others. "Let peace begin with me," tell yourself.

Whatever calls forth a strong reaction from you, be it person or situation, before you is your teacher: that very thing that upsets you is there for your good, to learn a lesson of non-reaction and non-power of appearance. "The stone the builders kept rejecting became the chief cornerstone of the building." (Matthew 21:42)

We grow in understanding to the degree that we can be aware of the tempter, knowing that it is a non-power. The power that it may seem to have is due to our resistance to it. To gain physical strength we must exercise, and the muscle fibers enlarge themselves and become stronger. So it is in the spiritual aspect of our being. We must use the temptation to enlarge the spiritual fiber within our being. They grow by an activity of grace beyond what the human mind can comprehend. Know well that the principle of growth comes from within the acorn, within the rose, and within you and me. It's called Life.

Any Truth or Principle proven one time anywhere in the universe is available to everyone. Again, God is no respecter of persons. There is hardly room to become puffed up with pride because I, of myself, can do nothing; that is, "I" as the personal sense of self, ego. The impersonal "I," which is God, does the work, as I am simply an instrument or branch of the vine.

These challenging experiences can be used as stepping stones on the path of enlightenment to True Identity. Many people see persons or situations as enemies that present as challenges that elicit strong emotional reactions within themselves. The only enemies that exist are of their own thinking, due to their attitude. Attitude represents an emotional state or mental condition which either blocks or facilitates the activity of God (good) expressing in their life experiences.

As stated earlier, there are no powers external to yourself to cause stress. Stress must be resolved or dissolved within your own consciousness by closing the department of worry in the mind. To do this one must evolve beyond the personal sense of self, the ego. Know that all things, persons, or conditions external to yourself are appearances perceived by the senses that tempt the mind to believe it is being threatened with extinction, ending the mind's existence. Because of this belief system operating, a defense mode of reacting is triggered. This is why personal sense of self, ego, always wants to be right. It, ego, equates being wrong, in its view and opinion, with dying. So it defends itself by judging, labeling and resenting. Peace of being is obscured or hidden under this false sense of existence. All discord of whatever nature will disappear from your experience to the degree of awakening to Truth.

Let the Light from the Lighthouse of Truth shine on you, in consciousness of Oneness. This is an All-Spiritual Universe. Being an all-spiritual universe would of necessity include my body, all forms of supply, the mind – All. The source and the substance are One. "I and my father are one," the Master Teacher informed humanity. It is up to each individual to awaken to that level of consciousness and cease judging from appearances, the environment of the senses.

All appearances and experiences are temporary, not Reality. Reality is eternal. The essence of all form and experience is Spirit, the only Reality. We speak of identical twins as a rarity;

we *all* are identical Spiritual Beings in temporary form, living the life of God.

THE PRISON OF FEAR, IGNORANCE

We always fear that which we do not understand. Most people are unaware of anything that the five senses have not informed the mind. The human mind, being finite or limited in scope, fears any uncharted sea of experience. This is part of the reason the mind seeks refuge in tradition, religions, conclusions or belief systems. An acronym for Fear is *F*alse *E*vidence *A*ppearing *R*eal.

The imprisonment of the individual is the limitation imposed by the mind and body, the mental and physical limitations of each. Beyond the mind and body, for most people, nothing exists. An active mind, filled with knowledge that it thinks it knows, is often not open for impartation and inspiration from within, from his True Identity, Spirit, his Source. This is a risk of formal education.

IMPERSONALIZATION

Far too many people feel that the manner in which they were influenced to view the world is the proper standard by which other people should view or judge the world. This is the source of much human conflict and misunderstanding, when and as an individual passes judgment from his or her point of view. After passing judgment, the individual then talks to the personal sense of self in his mind in support of the judgment that was made. In humanhood, there need not be a law or principle to support what is believed, beyond how he was influenced in earlier experiences of life.

After passing judgment, the energy of resentment arises within the mind that causes one to feel puffed up and very often to become impatient with the other person or circumstance. Feelings of resentment, unless one is aware, often move to anger with the person being resented and their behavior.

The resentment and anger, if unchecked, may lead to violence. Thus judgment and impatience trigger the emotion of resentment and anger. To curb violence, deal with the root cause, judgment and impatience.

Close the department of judging in your mind by knowing the Truth that makes you free of worry and anxiety. Your Truth Identity is forever free. Every tear shed is because of a sense of limitation in some aspect of your life. The personal sense of self knows duality of good and evil and always desires to improve or change the human experience. The Impersonal Self, Truth Identity, knows only fulfillment and completeness: "I and My Father are One."

Nothing is black or white except painting makes it so. Nothing of itself is good or evil except thinking makes it so!

When an individual personalizes what another says or does, the reaction is immediate. If you accept the unfavorable behavior of another as belonging to you, the reaction of judging, impatience and resentment manifests toward anger and violence.

To learn and practice choiceless *awareness* is a certain way to avoid the consequences of passing judgment of other people, whether individually or in groups. "IT IS AS IT IS." Those five two-letter words, when acknowledged and understood, provide a shield against personalizing another person's behavior as belonging to you.

Immediately the behavior becomes the past, a part of history. No one can undo an action that has taken place. Yesterday ended last night. The record written must stand. This *now* moment offers freedom of choice of your reaction or non-reaction. It will be the latter of the two if you simply acknowledge the *is-ness* of the moment without passing judgment, thereby remaining at peace.

The importance of crucifying the personal sense of self in order to cease judging and labeling is a lesson to ending the violence in the world and uncovering peace within individuals. This can only be realized by individual awakening to the consciousness of, "Peace, be still," silencing the mind of the "noise" of human thinking.

Become aware, know and understand that you are not limited by your past experiences, nor is your True Identity changed by experience. The impersonal "I" is unchanged and waiting to demonstrate its true nature of abundance in each person's life experience in harmony with an evolving level of conscious awareness of that individual, impersonally.

God is; "I am" is the Son of God *as* each one of us impersonally. We *appear* to be separate but, in knowing the Truth of the spiritual oneness of the universe, there is no separation from God nor each other in Reality.

To reach the place of impersonalizing your life experiences and achieve nonreaction, you must become choiceless aware of your thoughts and feelings in increasing moments throughout the day. Develop the awareness of the *is-ness* of the moment without judging good or bad.

There are many people who feel offended by another person's usage of a word, or expressing an opinion different than their own. As human beings we are challenged to control our own thought processes. We certainly do not have the ability to control another person. Whatever other people say or do, unless you personalize it as belonging to you, there is nonreaction. They are expressing at their level of consciousness and so are you. To accept their behavior as belonging to you triggers a reaction. Impersonalize it: "She said what she said," "he did what he did," "it is as it is," while being choiceless aware. Imagine another person observing that same situation or behavior without comment or physical reaction; *you* be that person.

There are 26 symbols that we call alphabets, which are arranged in a certain sequence to spell words. How can those symbols gain power over you to make you react unless you give them a false sense of power by reacting? Whatever is said or done is in the past. You are living in the "Now."

You cannot influence God nor mathematics by use of a multitude of words and thoughts. God's work is already complete, as is the principle of mathematics. Our assignment is to align, harmonize ourselves with that which is already complete.

The root of interpersonal violence and conflict is judging others and impatience. Recognizing the emotion of impatience as it is being born within yourself is the beginning of self-control. This is true even though you may have passed judgment on the behavior of another person.

Learning to forgive others becomes easy as you identify others with their ideal or True Identity. The Self of another person is the same Self that you are. There is one Self, God's Life expressing individually as each of us. To personalize as "my life" is to have a sense of separation, which leads to continuous conflict and ego growth. Remember, ego always wants to be right; resentment and anger is the habitual defense mechanism it uses to stay alive and active to wreak havoc in the perceived future.

POWER OF SILENCE

We have in our world endless testimony of the power and intelligence of Silence. Ponder the trees and the unique individuality of each leaf as is the uniqueness of every human fingerprint. All trees, natural resources, and sands of the sea appeared in Silence. In the Silence, the activity of amazing grace that the human mind cannot fathom, springs forth the infinite variety of forms and experience from the invisible realm.

Why worry about what you will eat, or wear? Seek first that kingdom of Silence, and the "things" will appear as needed. The peace that surpasses human understanding abides in the Silence.

The absence of evidence is not evidence of the absence of the intangible power which is omnipresent, omnipotent and omniscient that causes things to grow! The growth itself *is* evidence!

To silence human thought is to enter into the womb of silence, to uncover the missing peace and rest from human thinking. All human thought arises out of the false belief in two powers, good and evil, whereas in Truth there is one power which is omnipotent, omnipresent and omniscient: God, the Silent One.

Each of us has come into bodily expression from the invisible realm of existence to our present size and weight; all in silence from within. This is true of all life forms, both plant and animal, throughout the world. Why, then, doubt the power of Silence?

All human conflict would cease in the realization of this secret place of Silence. The political leaders of nations on earth could show, by example, the citizens of their respective countries the alchemy of this Silence. Then, there would be no possibility of wars and armed conflict. Peace on earth and good will toward man would become a growing reality. The pride of "me, myself and mine" is dissolved in the Light of the Womb of Silence.

The outer activity that an individual person is engaged in would continue, but with greater joy and gratitude by dwelling in the secret place of Silence through practicing living in the *Now* moment of awareness.

Ideas shall flow into the mind – ideas of expansion, growth, abundance and creativity – as the mind becomes void of human thought. From the Source of all creation these ideas emerge in silence. Any amount of words used concerning the intangible Silence remain just words until they are accepted into a fertile ground of consciousness; then the "ripple effect" will spread throughout the World community. "Let the silence begin with me," say to yourself.

THE HYPNOSIS OF HUMANHOOD: BELIEFS

To rise in consciousness, above that of humanhood is to "be in the world, but not of the world;" in other words, not to be governed by the universal belief in good and evil. The belief in good and evil is a hypnotic state which is the root cause of inharmony, discord, conflict, stress, sin, disease and lack.

The universal human belief in good and evil causes the missing peace in the experience of life of individuals. To unveil the peace, which is always present in Reality, requires an awakening from the hypnosis, just as one must awaken from hypnosis in the human scene to realize the rope is not a snake, or snakes are not growing in the flower pot.

Desiring that things or experiences be different, a dissatisfaction with what *IS*, trying to improve humanhood by new laws or whatever method, is proof of a belief in duality of good and evil. Spirit instructed Adam in Genesis 2:17 that, "the day that ye eat of the tree of knowledge of good and evil, that day ye shall surely die." What will we die to? We die to the understanding of oneness, no duality. This is an all-spiritual universe, and Spirit is God, One, with no opposite expressing Itself as form nor experience.

The missing peace shall be unveiled only in the silence of human belief in good and evil and realizing the spiritual oneness of the universe. The consciousness of humanhood shall never ever know peace. "My peace" is not of this world of the senses. The environment of the senses knows not peace. Be still and know I Am, God!

Judge not from appearances for that is to continue to live only from the environment of the senses, which are limited. In the silence of a belief in good and evil, there is no judgment, such as, "that's not right," "that's crazy, stupid," etc. Thoughts arise out of a system of beliefs that often become concretized through culture or tradition, the numbing influence of habit. According to your beliefs, it will be done unto you and appear as such in your experience.

Clearly, the veil that covers the missing peace is a belief in the duality of good and evil. One must dwell in "the secret place of the most high" by knowing the Truth of Oneness, no separation. This is an all-spiritual universe, only God exists. It appears to humanity according to beliefs.

To know and understand this Truth, one begins to live by the activity of Grace, without taking thought, just being a beholder of the unfoldment of that which is intended for individual unique life experiences. Human experiences are done unto each according to his belief. If "I" be lifted up (rise in consciousness of Truth) then one lives by the grace of God; not beliefs.

I have no life separate and apart from God. The real essential "I" that "I am" is one with the Source and Substance of my being. The substance of a thing is not separate from the thing itself. One cannot separate wetness from water, oak wood from the desk, for they are one.

The missing peace is at hand *Now;* it simply must be realized. All is in divine order based on one's belief. Inner peace stands knocking at the door of your consciousness. "Behold, I stand at the door and knock." (Rev. 3:20) Awake, thou that sleepeth, to the Spirit that dwells within your own consciousness, and be at peace, which comes from your Inner Self, "I."

Without the universal belief in duality of good and evil, there could never be a war or conflict between individual personalities. Teach the world the Truth of oneness. As a growing number of people are open and receptive to Truth teaching, the ripple effect or vibration will spread to heal the world of sin, sickness, war and a sense of lack or poverty.

Escape from the jailhouse of ignorance of oneness that the belief in good and evil has imposed on the mind. The imprisonment of the mind by beliefs does not allow the mind to be the avenue of awareness from the Inner Self, which remains at peace, eternally.

The number one priority is to uncover the missing peace within one's own being. Any discord felt within, whether it be worry, anger, resentment, frustration or whatever, is projected outwardly as a future life experience. It does not recede into the past, as man thinks it does, but serves as a source for future experience such as a movie projector is the source of activity on the movie screen. The sense world is the screen of consciousness.

A transformation of consciousness, from a discordant one to one of peace, is required for a joyous life experience to emerge. As within, so without. It is futile effort to change experiences without a change of consciousness. This is an unchangeable principle and one cannot fool principles or God.

Uncover the missing peace in order to have projected on the screen of life experiences joy, harmony, and fulfillment – to experience heaven on earth, which is God's gift to each of us.

An attitude of gratitude is the starting point that opens the gates to silence of mental activity. The environment of the senses constantly feeds the mind with information, seeming to block out silence and peace. The sense world of humanhood is so wide you can't go around it, so high you can't go over it, so low that you can't go under it. You must come in at the door of silence, prayer and meditation. To rely on the senses is to have the prodigal experience.

For most individuals to accept a transformation of consciousness will not be easy, for one must be sincere in the search for peace. The paralyzing influence of customs and tradition is a barrier that must be overcome and realized as a nothingness, a shadow. Your Truth Identity stands ready to be recognized, which is freedom from the hypnosis of humanhood. "Ye shall know the Truth, and the Truth shall make you free" of the paralysis of custom and tradition of the world. You then will be in the world, but not of the world of customs and traditions.

The Truth will also make you free of the universal human belief in duality, good *and* evil. The Kingdom of God need not be sought but simply recognized as already here *Now*.

Abide in the deep well of contentment, gratitude and joy, a state of consciousness that expresses itself on the screen of life experiences as peace, harmony, abundance and fulfillment of every need. The ripple effect of you and I dwelling in that lofty state of consciousness shall heal the World, one consciousness at a time, and then millions. If "I" be lifted up, all men shall be drawn onto Me, Peace.

In the allegory of creation Spirit, God, commanded, "Let there be light," and light manifested. Today, in human consciousness, there appears to be darkness, ignorance, at every turn of the page of human experience. Sin, sickness, poverty, violence and many other forms of inharmony and discord seem to cover the world of human existence as a direct result of this darkness of ignorance.

The word "ignorance" derives from the root word "ignore" and simply means a lack of understanding of Truth. To ignore Truth teachings is ignorance. Truth is not the same as facts. Truth never changes, cannot be amended or repealed. Mathematics is a Truth or Principle. What is a fact today can change tomorrow; not so with Truth. Mathematics remains the same in the world, as does the principle of aeronautics, because all principles remain unchanged.

Airplanes must fly according to the principle of aerodynamics to stay aloft and fly safely; otherwise, let me off of this plane! Fly the plane *the* way according to principle.

Inharmony and discord supplant peace in the mind and soul of millions of people in this world because of a lack of understanding of Truth; consequently, they are not free from the jailhouse of fear and ignorance. "Ye shall know the truth and the truth shall make you free" of fear and ignorance, and life experiences will be fulfilling and peaceful.

No matter at what financial price, peace cannot be bought, but it can be individually experienced by the silence of thought and stillness of the human mind. Peace you cannot find by using the human mind, because it is the human mind that is not at peace. A relaxation from the habit of the mind constantly entertaining thoughts must be reached in order to realize peace is already a part of one's Truth Identity. The goal is to become aware, know and understand that your Truth Identity is a light in the midst of humanhood's darkness of ignorance.

This is no simple task due to the incessant programming built into the fabric of society through the tradition of educational and religious indoctrination received since conception and birth into this dimension of existence.

This is an all-spiritual universe; therefore our Truth Identity is Spirit. The universal belief in being separate and apart from God or Spirit is the root cause of all human problems and the seeming absence of peace. We are one, spiritual. Another consequence of this belief in duality of good and evil is the pursuit of happiness by untold millions of people. Happiness "happens" and is a fleeting and temporary thing, depending on external circumstances, conditions and happenings. Instead of the pursuit of happiness, recognize joy to be one with inner Self. Whereas "happiness" is influenced by external factors, joy arises from within. The highway, expressway to joy is gratitude. In the midst of what may appear to be chaos to others, one can still be in joy (in joy in myself; enjoying myself). All forms of addiction – alcohol, tobacco, sex, food or religion – are seeking happiness and fulfillment in things external to one's self.

Peace and joy are twins, so to speak; when one is uncovered, there exists the other (they are really the same, just different words in describing the same thing).

You can experience happiness, and yet not be at peace with self nor others. Things, circumstances or conditions can be the catalyst for happiness, but never joy nor peace. Happiness results from stimulation of one or more of the five senses – *to* the mind and *through* the mind to the emotions. Happiness is of the mind, whereas Joy is of the Spirit.

All visible things are temporary of this world of form and experience; all shall pass from view. Several scriptural passages tell us, as relates to form and experience, "and it came to pass;" this too shall pass. Joy is a state of being, not an experience.

Certainly happiness is preferred over sadness and depression in the human realm, both of which are of the human mind. We must learn to let go of the lower realm of consciousness of humanhood to climb, ascend to spiritual awareness of individual Truth Identity of each of us. Just as in climbing a ladder, "you must let go of the rung below, there is no other way to climb, you know; you must let go of the rung below." The ripple effect of rising higher in conscious awareness of your True Identity shall be a blessing to other people who are ready to be awakened from the hypnosis of humanhood with all the lies that are built in by custom and tradition. Are you, the reader, ready to awaken further to the Truth of your Identity as a Spiritual being?

We are one with our Source, always have been, and always shall be. The belief in separation is the basis of the hypnosis of humanhood. The Source is the giver *and* the gift of Life. It is expressing Itself *as* the Self of me and you, oneness, no separation!

The misuse of the faculty of memory obstructs the realization of peace in the minds of far too many people in this world. Memory is a wonderful, divine gift but, like other gifts such as water, fire, electricity, etc., if misused it can or will destroy the user. Playing old tapes in memory of past experiences is a barrier to realizing the peace of the *now* moment. Many of those tapes are of the "somebody did me wrong song" type, thereby emitting negative emotions of resentment, anger or pride.

When the memory is active and the emotions associated with that past experience is nourished in the Now moment, seeds of similar experience in the future are being planted. Experiences unfold from states and stages of consciousness maintained by individuals. This is much like the screen at the movies. What is showing on the screen comes from the reel and projector. Our experiences are the screen, and the projector is consciousness. Unless there is a transformation of consciousness, experiences are unlikely to change. Remember, Psalm 127 begins: "unless the Lord build the house, they labor in vain that build." The Lord is your very own consciousness. Experience is the "house," consciousness unfolding! Hence, there are no victims, only volunteers.

By allowing the light of understanding to enter one's consciousness, the darkness of ignorance is evicted. Darkness can never survive in the presence of Light. As you are being the Light, illumination of that which is true shall be revealed and peace will thus be uncovered. Right now, Peace says in essence, "behold I stand at the door and knock." (Rev. 3:20)

To rely solely on the five-sense level of awareness is to be at a low level of consciousness. If "I be lifted up," i.e., if consciousness be raised to the level of understanding the spiritual oneness of the universe, peace is uncovered and God will be realized in the stillness and silence of words and thoughts in the mind.

The realization of peace is quite a challenge to the low level of human consciousness. That is why it is necessary to practice *awareness* at intermittent periods throughout the day. To do this does not present a burden but, on the contrary, will lighten any burden, tension or anxiety that may exist already.

I am aware that few people will end the habit of attempting to influence God by use of a multitude of words called prayer. Understand that true prayer is *listening* to the Word of God that is being imparted from within one's own consciousness in silence.

You are encouraged to withstand the momentum of habit of custom and tradition to take a new path to the kingdom of peace and joy. Wide is the path of tradition, and many travel on it, but narrow is the path that leads to peace; few there be who travel it.

This is often a lonely path where family and friends will not understand, because they are blinded by the traditions of the world of materiality, form and human experience. You will be a light where ever you go, for the Christ consciousness indeed glows in the oneness that Spirit is.

Judging, resentment and anger will be experiences of the past. You shall develop a love of your neighbor as yourself, in the awareness of oneness; I *is* one with my neighbor throughout the world, One, spiritual being.

To be the light of understanding, know well that it is not something to *get*. It is what you *let* emerge from within by, as Ralph Waldo Emerson said, "getting your bloated nothingness out of the way," which means surrendering that personal sense of self, the ego: "I die daily," Paul wrote. (I Cor. 15:31)

On the path toward enlightenment of truth and understanding, there will be many forms of temptation for you to leave the path and remain anchored in humanhood traditions. "Get thee behind me" is what the Master Teacher said to the tempter.

What did he mean by those words? As you face the sun, what do *you* know is behind you? Your shadow, of course. A shadow has no power, it is a *nothing*. As the Master faced the Light of Truth, all temptations were as shadows, thus the command, "Get thee behind me, satan."

We must not be less diligent in seeing all temptation to leave the path toward enlightenment as shadows, as nothing, without power. "That's a nothing," as Kehsi, the child, said.

Grow to the understanding that no person or experience has the power to take your peace. The unhappy feeling is in your mind because you have accepted something external to you as belonging to you; you have personalized the experience.

Practice being a beholder, a spectator of the *is-ness* of the experience, without writing a story in your mind *about* that which you observe. "It is as it is" are five two-letter words that will remind you of the *is-ness* of the Now Moment without judgment or impatience. By simply acknowledging the *is-ness* of the Now Moment you will affirm that nothing external to you has power to disturb your inner peace. "Judge not from appearance." Whatever information that the five senses gather for the mind is temporary at best. So return to wellness, peace.

The momentum of habit may continue for you to pass judgment and label things, persons and events for a while. Do not beat up on yourself. The very fact that you become *aware* that you did it again is a good sign that you are making progress in awakening from the hypnotic influence of external factors as having power over you.

Be a light in the midst of the darkness of ignorance in the world of humanhood. To be that light, know and understand that it is not anything that you *get*. It is what you *let* emerge from within. Go among them, but remain in the secret place of the Light by knowing the Truth of the Oneness of the Universe. In order to realize this state of bliss, one must place one's personal sense of self on the shelf. This means to surrender that personal sense of self, the ego personality that stands on a broad platform of ignorance and pride.

From the world of humanhood, with its pride, ignorance and ego, there comes the invitation to leave the path of peace and to rejoin the "party" of the world. These temptations are without substance or power.

Remember to tell yourself, "It is as it is," without writing a story in your mind about the person, event or situation. In other words, do not label or pass judgment, such as "that's crazy," "that's not right," "she's disrespecting me," etc. You react to the story that you write in your mind. You are now encouraged to simply be choiceless aware of the *is-ness* of that which you observe external to you. It does not belong to you.

Again, the momentum of habit of judging may be so strong that you may continue to label and pass judgment yet a while. Do not despair; start from where you are with a sense of gratitude that you are waking up from the mass hypnosis.

No matter the nature of the turmoil and storms of the world of humanhood, you will be able to see through the appearance to the Reality of Spirit and yet continue on your journey to knowing peace.

To be a Light of Peace requires the mind to be still from words and thoughts on a regular basis. One can learn to still the mind of words and thoughts by practicing awareness. In being aware, one is simply an observer, without choice of words; thoughts cease.

Let's repeat the awareness exercise by becoming aware of each finger on both hands, one at a time. Without looking at or moving the finger, become aware of each. Note that thoughts cease when you are simply being aware. The same effect ensues when one is being aware of one's breathing. Thoughts will come, due to the habit of the mind entertaining thoughts. Do not resist, just be aware of them, and let them pass as if a cloud is floating in the sky. The more you practice being aware, the more adept you become, as with anything that is practiced, voluntarily or involuntarily.

A mind that is relaxed from constantly thinking is open for inner direction from one's True Identity. The practice of awareness is used by many persons to *avoid* anger – not *manage*, but *avoid* anger. Learn to simply be *aware* of a behavior of another without judging, labeling or writing a story in your mind and you will begin to notice the "energy of resentment" subsides before it culminates or becomes the emotion of anger.

If there is a certain person whom you often have emotional reaction with, there before you is your Teacher. Observe the energy of resentment arising in you when that person comes to mind or in your presence. Your personal sense of self, the ego, judges and reacts with the emotion of resentment that oft times culminates in anger. Practice being aware without a mental conversation; simply notice the *is-ness* of the Now moment.

Go among them that you believed caused you to react, but remain in the secret place of a high consciousness by knowing the Truth of your True Identity is *one* with that other individual that *was* causing you to react. Again, that is your Teacher to become a light of peace in a world of discord and inharmony.

To be a light of peace in the world of darkness of humanhood, the mind must become still of words and thoughts. Human thought is based upon past experiences. The past, of course, cannot be undone, the record written must stand. The eternal *Now* moment presents an opportunity to rise in consciousness of Spiritual oneness of all that the senses observe.

As you develop the ability to live in the timeless *now* moment, you are uncovering the peace within Self. Time is an illusion. Again, today is yesterday's tomorrow; every instant from yesterday until today has been *Now*. The clock and calendar are human constructs, made for synchronicity of human activity. The calendar and clock are useful constructions, but the Truth of being is always Now. Every breath taken since birth has been and shall be *Now*. All living creatures – except human – all other living creatures, plants and animals are only aware of *Now*.

Come out from among the crowd of mass hypnosis of humanhood to be a light of peace. Focus on quieting the mind into stillness and awaken to God's eternal Light by learning to "think not" and live by grace, the givingness of God.

Although the world of humanhood will always show forth turmoil and problems, there is no need for anxiety and worry while secretly looking for happiness. Cease looking for happiness. Happiness "happens" and is fleeting and temporary. Some new experience "happens" to you in a *hap*-hazard fashion overshadowing your happiness, to an experience of unhappiness.

Whereas the human mind has accustomed itself to consider the past, present and future, these elements of clock and calendar intersect at the point where each breath is taken, the timeless moment of *Now*. Due to a lack of understanding, worry and anxiety blot out awareness of Now, where all is well. Take an extra dose of gratitude which will dissolve worry and anxiety and uncover the missing peace.

AGAIN, SEX, THAT HUSH-HUSH TOPIC

There are over eight billion people on earth; we all had our earthly existence begin by the union of a sperm from an adult male and an ovum or egg from an adult female. The activity that led to the union of sperm and egg is generally referred to as sexual intercourse between an adult male and female. There are many other terms used to describe this activity, some of which are only used in secret, perversely.

Far too few parents teach their children about sex and their sexuality, treating the topic as if it is taboo to discuss. Reflect on when and how *you* first learned. Was it from your parents, another adult or your young friends, playmates and buddies? Parents and adults usually avoid the sex topic if children are present. Yet, they, as parents, were all involved in sexual activity in secret that caused the child to be born.

Certainly sex can be discussed intelligently without using the "F," "pu" or "dk" words, or other smutty slang that refer to anatomy of the human body and its functions.

To talk of penis, vagina, clitoris, nose, ears or orgasm ought not to be beyond mentioning in a conversation, even if children are present. They are all body parts and functions.

God ordained the anatomy of humans, animals and plants. Why, then, should it be a taboo topic?

I surmise many men and women are imprisoned due to a lack of proper information on this topic of sex.

Certainly many unwanted pregnancies and abortions would be reduced if this topic were brought "out of the closet" and openly discussed with people old enough to understand the language of their culture.

Many personality disorders begin in utero, due to the feeling of rejection in unwanted pregnancies based in ignorance of sexual information.

Untold numbers of people, male and female, are locked in fear and anxiety due to errors in judgment based in addictions to the physical sensation of sexual activity.

Far too many people are ignorant of the spiritual aspect of sexual union wherein conception occurs, namely sexual intercourse between an adult male and female. To repeat, no man nor woman on earth knows how to make neither sperm nor egg. Spirit, God, is the Source of the cells which are necessary for the beginning of each of us eight billion people on this planet called earth.

Being consciously aware of the true Spiritual Identity of Self and one's sexual partner before and during coitus will imbue the new life form with a degree of spiritual awareness at birth that few individuals have experienced. History records the understanding and actions of a few of those individuals as miracles because so few parents are at a level of spiritual awareness at the moment of sexual activity that causes conception.

Conversely, many parents are altering the seeds of new life forms – sperm and egg – by being intoxicated from alcohol and other drugs. Certain aspects of society are deranged as a direct result of intoxication of one or both parents during sexual intercourse. The young, in addition to having open instruction on sexual topics, must be encouraged to not be intoxicated on *any* substance during sexual activity where conception is a possibility. A child conceived under such circumstances begins the human experience disadvantaged spiritually, mentally and physically.

"Namaste" is a Hindu or Sanskrit term recognizing the divinity within another individual. This recognition may be used, silently or verbally, at the beginning of sexual union wherein conception may take place. In one generation a seeming miraculous intervention, change, in the world (or society) will appear, dissolving much of the hodge-podge chaos we see today; thereby uncovering the missing peace within individuals and the world.

AWARENESS

There are few, if any, activities that an individual can practice that equals or exceeds in importance that of becoming aware. In the attitude of awareness, words and thoughts are absent. The individual is at a place of consciousness where the word of God is imparted from within. "Speak, Lord, thou servant heareth," is the mantra.

The momentum of habit, of the human mind entertaining thoughts, must be realized in order to enter the gates of awareness and simply become a beholder of all that the individual experiences. Judgment of these experiences that the five senses perceive as being good, bad or evil no longer persists in a state of awareness. The individual neither loves, hates nor fears the appearances of seeing, hearing, tasting, smelling or touching.

The tendency to pass judgment is arrested in that state of pure awareness. There is no longer the duality of good and evil. Whatever problem that was claiming to have power in your experience will dissolve into the nothingness from which it came, when being aware. In becoming aware, the mind becomes a transparency for that Inner Light to reach your receptive consciousness; the barriers of beliefs, and the thoughts produced by those beliefs, become still. The Light from within can come only to those who realize that it is already within each of us and each of us must find a way to let it escape. To prepare that way is through practicing awareness.

An excellent vehicle to use in the practice of awareness is to become aware of the unceasing activity of God in our individual life experiences. Be aware of the trees, flowers, animals without thought; be aware of your spouse or a friend, probably for the first time. Do not see them through the *image* of how you have come to know them in the past. If you do, you are not relating to them in the *Now*; they have changed and so have you.

Awareness is a wonderful tool to facilitate a transformation of consciousness, for out of consciousness of each of us does our own experience unfold individually. To endeavor to change life experiences without a transformation or change of consciousness is an exercise in futility.

Know that the Kingdom of God is within, (Luke 17:21) and each one of us must open out a way that this "imprisoned splendor" can escape. Through the avenue of awareness is the expressway to that place of peace, joy and fulfillment that those with human addictions are searching for; but they are searching external to Self through food, drugs, religion, sex or whatever form of addiction an individual experiences. Even with the addictions, an individual can learn to detach him/herself from such addictions by practicing awareness of the craving. By practicing awareness of the craving one can become aware that that craving is separate and apart from one's Self, for one's True Self is never addicted. The dissolution of addiction is like unto an alchemy of awareness that may appear as magical to the unaware person who is ignorant of the power of simply acknowledging the *is-ness* of the appearance without judgment as to good or evil; "it is as it is."

As awareness is achieved in the face of any appearance of problems, the mind becomes still and, in that place of stillness, something emanates from within which lights the way through, around or over the so-called problem that the human mind cannot fathom. That inner voice announces itself in silence, bringing understanding and peace. The evolvement to a new *is-ness* happens in secrecy and Silence.

This is an all-spiritual universe. Spirit is no respecter of persons. Becoming aware of the ceaseless activity of spirit is to pray without ceasing; for true prayer is beyond words and thoughts, to a listening to that still, small voice that utters Itself from within an individual when there is silence of human thoughts and beliefs.

What can mere humans tell God, an all-knowing entity that is omniscient, omnipotent and omnipresent? Yes, I understand what tradition tells us about prayer, but I am better served by listening instead of uttering a multitude of empty words that supplant awareness of the Inner Self. It is the self of the senses that believes that it profits by use of a multitude of words in prayer to try to influence God. Never believe that you know what to pray for. It is obvious that the world has not improved very much in thousands of years from that type of prayer that uses words and thoughts in an attempt to effect a change. Such attempts will always fail.

All attempts to have mathematics harmonize with a belief that 3+3=5 are as futile as an endeavor to influence God to come fix a certain condition or situation. Just as one must awaken to the principle of mathematics to get the correct solution that 3+3=6, so too must one awaken to experience God as omnipresent principle, and to harmonize with that principle, as is done in mathematics.

GRAINS OF TRUTH (WILL GROW WHEN RECEIVED IN FERTILE GROUND/CONSCIOUSNESS)

There have been many discoveries throughout history, tangible and intangible. One of the greatest *dis-cover-ies* in the intangible realm is the influence of attitude on individual life experiences. Ascending attitudes of appreciation, gratitude and praise have been found to uplift the spirit and feed the soul of the individual who dwells in these states of consciousness.

These attitudes of appreciation, gratitude and praise require the individual to be aware of the good that already exists in his/her life, and ponder (praise) the infinite invisible Source from which it comes into expression. It is the nature of humanhood to allow the mind to dwell on needs and wants that are unfulfilled. The thoughts are usually on what's missing or what could be better, or more.

Remember, it's not what you have lost or don't have, but what you have *left* that counts. Yes, count what's *right* with you, and that number will dwarf what's labeled as *wrong* in your experience of life.

The momentum of habit causes many people to be preoccupied with problems and complaints. This habit often leads an individual to feel that s/he is a victim and to begin to dwell in a descending attitude of self-pity.

If, in your humanity, you feel overtaken in a fault, take an extra dose of gratitude and then experience an immediate move toward joy and wellness. Yes, indeed, appreciation, gratitude and praise are expressways to greater good and optimism to dwell in your household of consciousness. If you are challenged to entertain these attitudes, become quiet, still the mind by practicing

111

choiceless awareness. This *Now moment*, become aware of each finger on your right hand without moving or looking at it. There is a subtle difference in *thinking* of your thumb and being *aware* of your thumb. In awareness, note the ceasing of thoughts!

When habitual thinking gives way to awareness, your True Identity of *"I"* can use the avenue of your mind to impart a light of understanding to dissolve any seeming darkness or problem that the mind has been entertaining. Every degree of greater understanding ought to be acknowledged with an increasing sense of gratitude. The activity of gratitude opens the portal through which evidence appears, causing even greater joy to be experienced, thereby washing away what seemed to be a problem. This happens much the same way as darkness disappears in the presence of light.

This power to transition experiences from gloom to joy is forever available. Absence of evidence of this power is not evidence of its absence. Ignorance, a lack of understanding, is the culprit in human consciousness. "Ignorance is the root of all misfortune." — S.B. Fuller

SUPPLY

Take a look at the nearest tree that you see. Is that tree real? Of course, it is a reality on this third-dimensional plane of humanity. Whatever is observed through any one of the five senses of seeing, hearing, tasting, touching or smelling is real on this material plane of existence.

Though the appearance of material objects, such as the tree, *seems* real to the senses, in Truth they are not Real. (All material form will change and disappear in time.) The form is not permanent but temporary, Reality is eternal. This human form of body is temporary, but that which is expressing Itself *as* body is infinite, invisible and eternal; *that* is Reality.

You may have been taught that money and what money can buy is your supply. It is in harmony with *TRUTH* to understand that neither money nor what money can buy is supply, but is the result or *effect* of supply. It is customary to use such terms as a supply of money, apples, oranges, food, etc. These all are the result or out-picturing of invisible Supply. Money, apples, or food may be gone but Supply remains because Supply is a law or principle in operation.

We may call that principle a law of God or a law of nature. The name we call it is not important, but the recognition or acknowledgement of a law operating to produce these things is important. Through the activity of grace, we experience from Supply, money, food and other forms according to our individual needs. We must acknowledge that Supply is infinite and invisible.

Paul, in the Bible, admonished us to look to the Source of good and not to look at "things;" 2 Cor. 4:18 says: "While we look not at the things which are seen, but at the things which are not seen: for the things which are seen are temporal; but the things which are not seen are eternal." Our True Identity, "I AM," is unseen, therefore to know and understand that "I Am *that* I Am" imparts a sense of freedom. One of the greatest problems in humanhood is that intangible feeling of incompleteness, of being unfulfilled. Gratitude and silencing of thoughts is the gateway to joy, not happiness, but joy that arises from within one's own self. Joy is unlike happiness that results from external influence of persons, places or things. The Infinite Invisible is the Source of all forms of supply and experience.

VICTOR OR VICTIM

"I Am" is the Source of all that I experience; there are no victims, only volunteers. My experience is my consciousness unfolding. To deny this principle is to play the blame game. This principle, understood, does not allow one to become a victim, even in the midst of increasing concern about the conflict and violence in the world.

Do you agree with the old saying: "If you are not a part of the solution, then you are a part of the problem."? Are you a light in a world of darkness? Are you open to dropping the conditioning and programming that you received from authority figures in your past? How often do you play the role of being the victim of circumstances?

Those individuals who participate in violent activity are essentially unhappy people who *believe* that they are victims of society. In a personal sense, they are right in regard to how they

113

have been conditioned or programmed to look outside of themselves for fulfillment and satisfaction. Many of them experienced conflict and violence in early childhood from parents and others who were looking outside of *themselves* for fulfillment. This was instruction for the child's conditioning and programming for future behavior. Added to this, we taught them that in order to feel good, or happy, someone must be made to feel bad, or unhappy. The emphasis to win over someone else teaches this lesson. In other words, "I will feel happy/good when I win over you," in some form of competition.

My life experiences and yours begin within our own individual consciousness; as within, so without. I am the Source of all that I experience. You are the source of all you experience. Although it may appear to be external, that is only an effect or result of an inner cause, Consciousness.

To have a change in experience from a feeling of being a victim, one must have a change of consciousness. This is not something to "get," but something to "let" evolve from within your own being by stilling and silencing the mind of its many beliefs and concepts.

Human thinking is based upon the false belief of duality, good and evil. "The day that ye eat of the tree of knowledge of good and evil, that day ye shall surely die." What will you die to? One dies to the knowledge and understanding of spiritual *oneness* of the universe, no duality.

God, mathematics, gravity or any principle is no respecter of persons. As hard as it may be to accept by some, each of us is responsible for our own experience; as within (our individual consciousness), so without (our life experiences); consciousness unfolding!

Playing the victim role may be self-fulfilling to the ego-self. As you believe, so be it unto you. "It is done unto you as you believe." (Matt. 8:13)

The personal sense of self finds it easy to blame factors external to itself, not understanding that there is an aspect of Self unknown to the human mind. Be still and know "I Am," your Inner True Identity and be free of the victim mentality.

That negative feeling of being a victim is arising in the individual, not outside as one might suppose. It comes from a belief system that is not founded on Truth. As one believes, so it is unto one's self. No event, experience or person has the power to make you have that unhappy feeling of being a victim when you know the Truth that makes you free! That freedom cannot be described. That would be like describing how an orange tastes to a person who has never tasted an orange. Words would be inadequate in both cases. Truth cannot be put into words. Be silent; drop the hypnotic belief system and Truth appears in consciousness and manifests outwardly by an activity of grace.

The point of playing the victim role is based on what the individual thinks and feels in the mind, never able to admit that maybe his judgment is lousy, preferring to blame others, situations or things.

As Nelson Mandela responded when asked, "How does it feel to be free after 27 years?", "I was always free." Freedom from the mindset of being a victim is a personal choice. One ought not free himself from accepting responsibility for his lot in life now and in the future. The individual is responsible. Just as a seed knows its destiny, so does a state of consciousness know its projection on the screen of life experiences. An acorn knows its destiny is an oak tree, not an apple, peach or pine tree. Consciousness out-pictures itself by an activity called grace.

To shatter the illusion of being a victim, learn to live in the *Now* moment, not past nor future; grace will then be found to be sufficient in ways we know not.

"I" IS A PRINTOUT OF THE DIVINE

There (here) is a reason we all call ourselves individually by the same name throughout our lives of human existence. Yes, our parents gave us names for them and others to identify and call us; that is why others and my parents call me Lewis Carter Baskins. But I do not call myself by that name. I call myself, *"I."* I call myself by the same name that you call yourself for a very good reason, that reason being that there is only one Self manifesting or expressing Itself in an infinite variety of forms. Being told to "love your neighbor as yourself" is on target because, in Truth, your neighbor *is* yourself, the One Self individualized. Is it by instinct that everyone, when referring to him or herself, calls themselves

"I?" Do you not feel and say "I" within your mind throughout the waking hours of the day and when speaking to another? Be clear, the human mind only knows the personal sense of "I" (me): "I of mine own self can do nothing." (John 5:30) The eye, foot, hand, of themselves can do nothing without the Inner Self, "I," being in charge of their actions. The personal sense of "I" is as an "arm of flesh," without power.

There is only one Self *appearing* as several billion individuals on earth. The five senses can only inform the mind with *inform*-ation that is limited, for the senses are limited in perception. Beyond the horizon of the senses is infinity and eternality of *Now*. Present-moment awareness is the gateway to this realization.

What answer comes to you when you ask of yourself, "Who am 'I'?" What is this thing called "I?" Am "I" to be found in my mind? Feet, nose, from the bottom of my feet to hair on my head, where am "I?" Am I my body? No. "I" *have* a body, a mind, etc.

Who is living your life? Is it what Daddy taught you? Mama? Who taught you what you believe? Who's doing the listening and talking when you are in a conversation with others? Are you judging what you hear through the screen of what you think you already know? If so, then you are not listening. Is that your father or mother listening?

This is the fate of many individuals who see themselves as victims in life, instead of victors. "I" is one with the Creator. We listen to It in prayer or meditation. Again, prayer is not talking to God, but having a listening attitude, even in all outer activities in which we may be engaged. "I" will be with you always from the appearance on earth *as* a sperm and egg, that no human on earth knows or understands how to consciously make, but "I" do.

The personal sense of self, the mind of each individual, is that aspect of humanhood that feels incomplete, separate and apart from others. This *sense* of separation is the basis of the feeling of incompleteness. We are One because this is an all-spiritual universe. There is not Spirit *"and,"* or God *"and."* There is no *"and;"* only God *is*.

Yes, there are many beliefs, concepts and appearances that tempt humanity to accept a sense of separation from Oneness.

Remember what the master said to the temptations? "Get thee behind me." As we face the Light of Truth of Oneness, so-called problems are as shadows that have no power. They *do* appear but are without power of any kind. We are encouraged to "judge not from the appearance" of things.

LITTLE THINGS MEAN A LOT

After traveling by foot across a country over a desert, rivers, mountains and valleys, the traveler was asked by media, what gave him the greatest problem? The rivers? The mountains? The desert? The answer to all such questions was, "No." Then what was it, Mr. Matthews, that gave you the most problems? Immediately came the response, "It was the little pebbles that kept getting in my shoes."

We often prepare for the big challenges in life by getting an education, developing a savings plan, raising a family and other traditional things. Why, then, is there so much unhappiness and chaos in the world today? It is the little things that the world of the five senses ignores due to not being aware.

In reading of these ideas being expressed on this printed page, the space that separates each word is important for easier reading than having all the words strung together such as (havingallthewordsstrungtogether). These spaces between each word represent silence.

In the environment of the senses, the sense world or human experience, there is little or no silence. The senses constantly inform the mind with *inform*-ation that can be described as noise of the senses because it blocks out silence from constant thoughts being entertained in the mind. "Man shall not live by bread alone, but by every word that proceeds out of the mouth of God." (Matt. 4:4) Silence is the mouth of God.

Learning to listen from within to one's own being, to the words (ideas) being imparted, is true prayer of listening to God, not talking to God. What can a human state of consciousness tell an omniscient, all-knowing entity we call God?

Another "little thing" that means a lot is, as mentioned earlier, the custom and tradition of referring to young people by the same word that we call young goats, i.e., "kids." I know there are successful adults in many walks of life that were referred to as "kid" when they were children. My point being, if *any* child is affected adversely by being called other than a human, that "little thing" ought to be abandoned. I'm not suggesting that the word, "kid," alone, causes damage to all personalities, but why run the risk of damaging a young mind? As I grew up in Arkansas, I observed that in cutting a tree down with the axe, it was not only the last blow that felled the tree, it was *all* of them. In a similar sense, there are many influences that shape a personality. I think this is one of the blows that adversely affect some young people, boys, girls, students, children, nieces, nephews.

A "bitch" is a dog. That is an offensive word to call any person. Why call young people by any other animal name? If it's an individual child you are speaking to or about, does s/he have a name that you are aware of? Use the name, not "kid." At what age or level of development does a young person cease being a "kid?" Is it arbitrary to the speaker or is it legal?

Are children beasts or animals? How about lending young people some dignity by calling them "young man," "young people," "young lady," "Mr." or "Miss," and not by using the same word as we call animal, i.e., "kid." Little things mean a lot. Be done with the paralyzing tradition of referring to young people as "kids," please.

Another "little thing" that custom and tradition have the world hypnotized is use of the three words, "I am sorry." Parents often teach children to declare themselves to be "sorry" and, as a result, the child may grow up to be what the world calls "sorry." "Tell him you are sorry," many parents say to their children. Do you really desire your child to be a sorry person?

"Excuse me," "pardon me," "forgive me," "my bad," "I apologize" or other expressions of admitting an error or mistake (which all humans make) seem more appropriate in lieu of declaring one's self to be "sorry." "I," your Truth Identity, is *never* sorry.

"I am" are two powerful words, for what you put after them shapes your reality. To use the words, "I am," followed by anything unlike good (God) is to use the Lord's name in vain. Avoid using terms such as "I am tired," "broke," "sick," "angry," "miserable;" to do so is to feed the ego because the ego enjoys misery. If the ego cannot find inharmony, it creates it.

I am aware that when such terms are used, it is the personal sense of self (ego) that is spoken of; however, we are speaking of many "little things that mean a lot." Because it is the personal sense of self that has human experiences, the impersonal "I" of your Truth Identity is always perfect, whole and harmonious. "Before Abraham was, I AM." (John 8:58)

I understand that the momentum of habit will keep many "little things" in use no matter the cost in terms of human experience for "this is how I was raised," as if to say the authority figures in one's early life were in harmony with the laws and principles that govern righteousness *(right-use-ness)*.

Another "little thing that means a lot" is when speaking before a group of people or to an individual person is the hedging of remarks by announcing what you "would like" to do or "want to do." The natural question to ask is, "When?" You announced what you would like to do, so when? Many speakers feel a sense of gratitude and say, "I would like to thank ___," or "I want to thank ____." Since you ae speaking, why announce what you "would like" to do? Go ahead and thank them *now*. "I thank you," not "I want to thank you," or "I would like to..." The speaker would become a much more effective speaker if s/he would stop hedging these "thank you" remarks by commenting, "I would like to."

"You know what *they* say" is sometimes used to persuade another person to conform to custom or tradition. Who are *"they?"* Why did *they* say or do it? Was the circumstance the same? Be encouraged to listen from within; listen to your inner guidance, that small voice that utters itself from within your own being. Never mind what *"they"* say. "They" said that the bumblebee is not supposed to fly; the wingspan is too short for the weight of the body, but the bumblebee didn't go to school to learn what *they* say, so it keeps on flying.

Individuals sometime pay a cost for following the crowd. You can be *in* the world but not *of* the world of customs, and traditions. It's OK to be different from the crowd.

Little things mean a lot, for they are what the big things are composed of. A rose is beautiful to look at, but the details of that rose are fascinating to observe in its perfection, even down to the smallest petal that may appear or a tiny seed. All show forth in silence by an activity of grace, of spirit or God, bringing forth the visible from the invisible realm. All things visible emerge out of the invisible in silence. "Call no man on earth your father." The Invisible is (y)our Father.

PEACE, BE STILL

"Let not your heart be troubled, neither let it be afraid." (John 14:27)

That feeling place of incompleteness and discontent that many individuals nourish is a direct result of the universal human belief in good and evil. That belief carries with it desires other than the Now moment. For each individual, this Now moment is as it must be according to that individual's state of consciousness.

Consciousness out-pictures itself much like a movie screen reflecting the images from the reel and projector. The images perfectly reflect the reel and projector; to change the images that appear as life experiences, there must be a transformation or change of individual consciousness.

Consciousness is transformed not by might, nor by power of the individual person, but by letting the mind be still and empty of human beliefs and concepts that are passed on by custom and tradition.

How can the mind be still of beliefs and thoughts? Many people have difficulty in falling asleep because the mind is making so much noise as thoughts. Many of those thoughts are of the nature of playing old tapes in memory of past experiences, even all the way back to childhood. Learn to live where life eternally exists, in the *Now* moment.

Let us now repeat the *awareness* exercise to assist in realizing the *Now*. It is suggested that you *pause* after each question in order to experience an answer to the question being asked.

Here go the questions:

Without looking or moving it, how do you know that your left hand exists? (pause) The moment the question was asked, you became *aware* of your left hand. Now that we have established what "awareness" is, become aware of your thumb on your right hand. (pause) Now the middle finger on the left hand. (pause) Do you notice a feeling of calmness by coming into the Now moment?

All sound arises out of silence and returns to silence. For the next minute or two, become aware of any sound you hear and endeavor to be aware of the silence beneath the sound. (pause) Again, be aware of middle finger of your left hand. (pause) If you were successful in being aware of your finger, there was nothing else going on in your world, past nor future, was there? (pause) Now you were not *thinking* of your finger, you were simply *aware* of it. In being *aware,* thoughts cease to exist and calmness ensues.

Notice the peace and quiet that was felt as you came into awareness of the *Now* moment.

Coming into the *Now* is also experienced when one becomes aware of his or her breathing, or the spoon on the table, anything.

While practicing being aware of each of your ten fingers or breathing, thoughts *will* come into the mind, due to the momentum of habit of the mind entertaining thoughts. Do not resist them, just let them pass as clouds floating in the sky, and return to practicing being aware. Anyone improves through practice, so be patient with yourself.

When the mind is quiet and still, peace reveals itself and the mind becomes an avenue for your Inner Truth Self to communicate with the outer personality. Just as no one can breathe or digest your food for you, so it is in allowing a transformation of consciousness. Each individual must allow that transformation. Do you see that?

ANGER AVOIDANCE

Experiences of person, situation or condition do appear and tempt us to resist, pass judgment and experience anger. We, too, can say within ourselves individually, "get thee behind me, tempter; you are as a shadow without any power." Only as we learn to face the Light of Truth are we imbued with such power. To use the faculty of *awareness* of the person, situation or condition is to remain at peace.

You are hereby encouraged to accept as your consciousness those five two-letter words: "It is as it is." Some say, "It is what it is," which essentially means the same thing, but I prefer five *two-letter* words, "it is as it is."

What someone says or does has no power to make you angry. "S/he made me so angry," simply is not a true fact. What caused the anger is what you said to yourself *about* their behavior, *judging* what s/he said or did. It is your self-talk to which you are reacting. As you change your inner conversation from one of passing judgment and feeling the energy of resentment that begins to arise in you, to simply being *aware* that s/he said what s/he said (or did), "it is as it is." Do not accept their behavior as belonging to you by passing judgment.

Remember the exercise of being *aware* of your thumb? By using the same faculty of *awareness*, become aware of any resentment feeling whenever it seems to arise in you; then notice it begins to immediately dissolve into its native nothingness. As resentment disappears, the firestorm emotion of anger is avoided. That resentment-causing behavior is history, past: Yesterday ended last night. The moving finger writes and moves on; your anger, reaction or tears will not wash out one word of it.

As you learn to simply acknowledge the *is-ness* of an experience, without passing judgment or labeling it based upon your past experience, you will reduce the energy of resentment that arises in you. That resentment culminates in anger and sometimes violence.

Whatever the experience – "s/he said what s/he said" (it is as it is), "s/he did what s/he did," (it is as it is) – do not write a story in your mind (judgment) *about* the experience. You react to the story you write. "That's crazy," "He's disrespecting me," "That's not right," "I'm sick and tired of ___," etc. What another person does or says has no power of itself, until you give it the illusion of power by passing judgment, labeling and resisting it.

Be aware of their behavior, yes, but do not accept what is said or done as belonging to you. Simply be aware; be a beholder of "it is as it is." Do not personalize their behavior as belonging to you. "This, too, shall pass," one should realize.

Everyone that practices being aware of "it is as it is" sees a difference in a short period of time. Instead of reacting with resentment and anger, they avoid *reacting* and are able to choose a *response*. Often the response is no response, only silence.

One will begin to understand things never understood before and be relaxed. Learn to discern; simply be aware; don't judge. Become aware of how not to mix emotion with that which is being observed with the senses. All things observed with the senses are of the past. To see lightning and hear thunder are of an event already happened; the clash of negative and positive energy discharged from clouds.

To see or hear the behavior of another is of the past. Why react to events of the past? It is as it appears to be. Do not accept it as belonging to you, do not personalize.

Know and understand this: we all behave the best we understand in the state of mind or level of consciousness we are in at the moment the behavior is exhibited. What, then, is the justification for each of us to pass judgment on another? Communicate without emotion, yes, but cease reacting and judging.

The root cause of violence is passing judgment and impatience. Grow to become aware of that energy of resentment as it begins to rise in you when you judge others. As you become aware of that energy of resentment it will immediately begin to subside. It cannot survive the light of awareness and observation.

The paralyzing influence of custom and tradition, and the momentum of habit will lead one to violate one's own integrity for yet a while. You are encouraged to begin, and the ripple effect will go out from you to benefit others as they touch the hem of your consciousness.

Remember, "It is as it is," and other people's behavior does not belong to you, so cease accepting it and there will be no reaction set on automatic. As consciousness grows, you can choose a response without reacting. Now you are growing in avoiding the emotion of anger and learning to love others as yourself, your Truth Self within.

A lack of understanding is called ignorance. All humans are born into a world of ignorance. Formal education simply polishes one's ignorance and, far too often, one comes out of such training being a sophisticated ignoramus, not awakened to one's True Identity. Many of these same people gain positions of "authority" that mislead the masses into further hypnosis of humanhood.

Realize and know that all is well. In Reality, all is eternally well. No human experience in the history of mankind effects a change in that wellness or wholeness of Reality. Individually, you can awaken to the consciousness of wellness that is, at this moment, closer than your breathing, nearer than hands and feet. The chaos, confusion, conflicts and problems in the world today are not of the Reality of Wellness of which we speak. This Reality can never be recognized by those caught up in the madness of the world. How can one describe the color green to a man born blind?

You have a choice of awakening to the Truth of Wellness or of passing the illusion along to future generations, your replacements on Planet Earth. Choose ye this day, whom or what you shall embrace. You shall know Truth and Truth shall make you free from passing judgment, resentment and anger.

Be clear: to react emotionally to an experience is to relive the experience. The prefix, *-re*, is to do over again, as in redo, retrial, remake. So, when you *re*-act, you live the experience again and again in your mind. Remember, this experience has already happened; it is in the past, a part of history.

THE UNCHANGING REQUISITES OF LEADERSHIP – S. B. FULLER

1. Initiative (to begin)
2. Courage (to overcome obstacles)
3. Integrity (to live without pretending)
4. Loyalty (to remain true)
5. Perseverance (to persist) – Failure is not the falling down, but a refusal to get up

EDUCATION PROCESS – S. B. FULLER

1. Observation
2. Concentration
3. Memory
4. Reason
5. Action

BEYOND THE HORIZON

Appearance and form is my horizon. As I look out across the lake, there is a point where the sky and water appear to come together. Should I travel to that point by boat and again lift my eyes, there is another point in the distance where water and sky appear to meet. The point beyond which I cannot see is my horizon.

The same phenomenon appears as I look down railroad tracks. In the distance, the parallel tracks appear to come together as one. If this was accepted as true fact, no one would ever board a train to travel great distances.

These illustrations should demonstrate to us not only the limitations of the five senses, but also the limitations of that which we "see" as relates to understanding ideas: "Oh, now I see" is what we say when an idea becomes clear to us that was a bit fuzzy in our mind.

In an endeavor to overcome some of the problems and challenges in our human experience of life, we may not see our way forward clearly. Sleepless nights, tension in the shoulder, a frown on the brow are often symptoms of not "seeing" clearly.

Sometimes all of one's thinking, planning and scheming do not seem to be sufficient to move past the problem. You see, all human thought and planning is based on previous experiences; so to be as a hamster, going around and around in circles will not solve nor dissolve the problem of your little world. In many cases, past experiences do not offer a clue for the solution of the problem, so the feeling of discontentment persists. Be clear, however; all problems do have a solution, otherwise it would not be a problem. The solution may not be found in our past experience, however.

It is well to be aware, to know and to understand that, "beyond the horizon of my little world, there is a great big world." – S. B. Fuller

Our "little world" consists of past experiences and present awareness. 1 Cor. 2:9 tells us, "Eye hath not seen, nor ear heard, neither have entered into the heart of man the things which God hath prepared for them that love him." Now, if neither eye nor ear has observed the solution to the problem, that means it is not a part of (y)our past experience.

Often, it is an exercise in futility to humanly plan and take thought for some problems. One must arrive at the state of consciousness where one "takes no thought" for the problem, whatever its nature, and lives by Grace, the unfoldment of the gifts of God in silence without thought. Man shall not live by human experience alone, but by every word that proceeds out of the mouth of God. The "mouth of God" is Silence; Silence the belief in good and evil, which is a universal human belief.

Trying to change or improve humanhood from the *is-ness* of now in order to satisfy an inner feeling of discontent and unfulfillment, consumes the life span of all but a few humans. Those few who are not consumed have begun to awaken to the Truth of being, and live by the grace of God.

The Infinite Invisible Source of all form and experience responds to states and stages of human consciousness because there is no separation of consciousness and life experiences. Experience is simply consciousness unfolding. Do you see that?

Beyond the horizon of my little world, there is a great big world, an invisible world awaiting acknowledgement by individualized consciousness of who-so-ever will open themselves to Truth principles.

As problems arise, the question is, "How can I meet it?" You search your memory of past experiences for an answer, only to find emptiness. We must still the mind and "let" the solution be revealed to us in silence from that infinite invisible realm wherein *all* things are known. This is true prayer, *listening* to God, not *talking* to God. Again, what can mere humans inform an omniscient, all-knowing entity, God?

As we get to know this spiritual principle we begin to see the problem dissolve, a confirmation of, "Ye shall know the Truth, and the Truth shall make you free" of the problem.

So, "Be still and know I Am, God," the Infinite Invisible. Let the mind be an avenue for ideas to enter from the Source, the Infinite Invisible, to dissolve problems, to remove the illusions of lower consciousness.

We are encouraged in scripture to judge not from appearance but to judge right. Right Judgment comes from knowing, understanding and being aware that this is an all-spiritual universe. The appearance, form, is my horizon, the limited human consciousness that perceives with the senses and from memory of past experiences.

There ought to be no despair because in the Infinite Invisible realm wholeness, wellness and fulfillment endure eternally. Note how Paul in his writing affirms this point of focus, in spite of appearances. (2 Cor. 4:18) In the horizon state of consciousness, we do become attached to form and experiences, all of which are temporary in their existence. These forms and experiences include people, places and things.

All of us were born into this parenthesis (-) by parents, mother and father. We are encouraged in scripture, however, "to call no man on earth your father." Yes, we came *through* our mother but we most certainly did not come *from* our mother. She was the avenue or instrument of That which is unseen, used for our arrival on this plane. No man nor woman on earth consciously knows how to make a sperm or egg. The mother knows not how to make a liver, kidney or toenail. All organs were formulated from the Infinite Invisible realm by an activity of grace, the givingness of the Source, which is beyond the horizon of human understanding.

THE PURSUIT OF HAPPINESS

Joy in life does not result from the presence of something outside of ourselves; it is the absence of something within ourselves. For example, gloom is a state of inner blocking of the Light of our True Identity; joy is the release of gloom. Just as a balloon rises higher by discarding weights, so does one ascend in joy as one discards negativity. Happiness is always temporary. Joy, however, is eternal as the sun is eternal; though one may not now experience the sun, it still exists beyond the horizon of my present vision, as does Joy.

Of what merit is happiness while there is yet an inner discontent? Happiness *hap*-pens by chance or accident; it depends on outer experiences of the past. It is fleeting, never stable or lasting: "She said *this* and I was so happy;" "She said *that* and I was unhappy;" "I got a new car and I was so happy until someone hit it and I was unhappy." You see, happiness has an external cause, whereas joy arises from within.

Anyone can experience Joy. No matter what may appear to be chaos to others, one can still be in joy (enjoy). The expressway to joy is an attitude of gratitude. Joy is uncaused. It unfolds naturally by an activity of grace from the Infinite Invisible realm, in an atmosphere of gratitude. Learn to dwell in a deep well of gratitude, contentment and joy. Suddenly you will find that no one has the power to hurt nor offend you anymore; peace is thereby uncovered.

When an individual develops the habit of reacting in resentment and anger to the behavior of others s/he experiences, in essence they communicate a message that says, "Change what you said or I will hurt myself by becoming angry;" "If you don't stop doing that I will hurt myself again and again." "I want to change your behavior so that I can feel good." Foolish, don't you think?

That attitude smacks of one who feels powerless, while at the same time having connection to the Source of all power within himself. Ignorance of this connection is the hallmark of the world of humanhood. Yes, learn to be *in* the world but not *of* the world. In lieu of reacting, simply acknowledge the *is-ness* of the moment and recognize this as an opportunity to learn and/or teach others in the ways of righteousness. This must start somewhere; why not with you and me?

To uncover the missing peace in a situation or circumstance is not by might nor by power but by being still and silent of mind in order for the mind to be an avenue of awareness of the *is-ness* of the now moment and be open to the impartation from within for solution ideas. Then, you shall be moved from a world of discontent to a deep well of contentment and gratitude. The Infinite Invisible is here, Now.

ILLUSIONS

As humans, we are born and raised to sleepwalk through life experiences, clinging to illusions until, among some of us, there is a partial awakening to having been indoctrinated, programmed and conditioned by society, this world. The chief goal of society, it appears, is to keep society sick and sleepwalking.

This hypnotic influence exerts its power in subtle ways, beginning in utero of pregnancy, through mental and physical diet fed to the mother. The unborn child is one with the mother. It "eats" what Mom eats. It feels the emotions of Mom. It "sees" what Mom sees.

It's important for young people of child-bearing age to understand that the unborn child is being molded, to a significant degree, in other ways in addition to physical development. The mother who experiences lots of anger during pregnancy usually sees a baby that cries and frets much more than other siblings where such anger didn't exist during those pregnancies. A feeling of insecurity is due to illusions of lack in the universe that is being passed on to the unborn child, who will experience lack in his/her life as consciousness unfolds into experience.

We can readily see the responsibility of the father to assist the pregnant mother to be calm, serene and joyous during the months of gestation, pregnancy. Whatever the prevailing mood of the mother, it will be reflected in the child. Most often that trait is carried into adulthood until there is a transformation of consciousness within the individual.

As relates to consciousness, the transformation is being "born again," which every individual has the opportunity to experience as s/he grows in understanding of Truth, which dissolves illusions. We are told in biblical scripture, "Ye shall know the Truth and Truth shall make you free" from the inherited hypnotic influences of humanhood.

Many adults now feel a continuous sense of unfulfillment and discontentment that they have been unable to identify or overcome. In many cases it is inherited, and it shall continue until there is a transformation of consciousness.

The illusion of time causes much stress in the human family. The calendar and clock are useful human constructs, to be sure. If you were to ask that tree outside your window, "What time is it?" the answer could only be, "Now." Now is the only time! Again, today is yesterday's tomorrow; every instant between has been Now.

Every breath taken, since being born into human form, has been *Now*. We never breathe for five minutes past or yet to come, but only *Now*. To realize and focus attention *Now* is to live as on the cusp of a wave in the ocean. In the *Now* moment, all is well.

The momentum of habit of the mind to entertain thoughts of the past, in that faculty called memory, is the source of much inharmony in the life experience of individuals.

Memory is a wonderful divine gift. When misused, however, it will destroy. Fire, water, electricity are all wonderful gifts but each of these will destroy when misused. The concept of past, present and future is programmed into a child at an early age. The influence of previous experiences limits individuals in discovering and living their purpose for having come to this parenthesis.

To remove the restricting influence of previous experiences, the illusion of linearity (past, present, future) must be shattered. The continuous presence of *Now*, to those who understand clearly, shatters the belief in "birthday" celebrations. Just as this present day will never come again, the day of his birth will never return again. According to the calendar that humans created, it is the "anniversary" of his birth, but it certainly is not his *birthday*. The illusion created by man in the creation of the calendar and clock keeps us occupied with the concept of time; therefore few people are aware of the *Now* moment where peace is found or uncovered.

To not live in the eternal now is the state of those who see themselves as victims, living in dread of the future and in the shadow of the past. The "victim" thus is the creator of his negative experiences in life, but he always looks external to himself for a victimizer, which is himself, surprisingly.

The illusion of power has many people seeking to possess certain positions in their lives. God is the only power to seek. That power is available to all that sincerely seek without ego but with humility.

One of the greatest illusions of humanhood is a belief in death. Life was never born nor will life ever die because Life is God, the eternal, Infinite Invisible. My life is God's life individualized as me.

All form and experience are temporary. That tree outside your window one day will not be there but that which is expressing Itself *as* tree, you cannot see that. That is Life, God, the Infinite Invisible. We "die" to being a child in becoming an adult, just as the caterpillar dies to become a butterfly.

The word "death" is applied to the action of all energy appearing to leave the physical body and it is seen as an ending to life, but it is no ending, only a forward movement into another parenthesis (-).

The essence of an individual spirit does not cease to exist. It continues to express Itself in other dimensions that are just as real as the senses now proclaim in this dimension.

Birth into this dimension is death from a previous dimension of existence, as "death" from this dimension will be birth into yet another dimension of expressing Spirit, which we all are in essence. This dimension is a parenthesis (-) in eternity.

The caterpillar makes a transition in form, yet it is the *same* life, only a different form.

Another illusion is to believe that any person, situation or circumstance external to you has any power to stress you or make you angry. Stress and anger are inside jobs, they arise from within your mind based on your "self talk," what you say to yourself in passing judgment. "Judge not by appearances."

Your false self, ego, sets a standard of perfection in the mind, and when it perceives that someone violates that standard, it judges and reacts with resentment, then anger.

The fact is that there is nothing external to you that has any power of itself to cause any emotional reaction. It's the belief that it does have power that causes one to experience resentment and anger.

The onset of an individual not being at peace is due to the mind believing and accepting the illusion of time by remembering the past or being anxious about the future, whereas *living in the now* allows peace and serenity to reveal one's True Being.

In the beginning is the Word and the Word becomes (World) flesh.

Word	Work	World
(idea)	(activity)	(experience)

SELF RELIANCE

Biblical scripture (Psalm 24:1) tells us, "…the earth is the Lord's and the fullness thereof; the world and they that dwell therein." The earth that we humans know as a planet is not separate and apart from the oneness of Spirit, God; this is an all-spiritual universe. "In the beginning God (Spirit)…" (Gen. 1:1) Thereafter, all form and experiences are of the one essence, God (Spirit). We are eternally in coexistence with God.

The word earth is also used in reference to material forms and experience which are effects of an earlier cause. We have heard of "the law of cause and effect" which is analogous to the law of "sowing and reaping" that was referenced earlier in this book. The sowing and reaping reminds us that "every man must bear his own burden." (Gal. 6:5) Individually everyone is manufacturing his own future, for consciousness unfolds as experience.

"The earth is the Lord's" helps us to understand that the world of form and experience of each of us is the unfoldment of individual consciousness which is the Lord. Consequently, the Lord of an individual's world of experience is that person's consciousness. This is the reason why each individual's world of experience is uniquely different from another; just as fingerprints are unique to an individual, so is his world of experience.

The collective consciousness of a community, nation or society is molded and influenced by the customs and traditions of that group. Thus, as an increasing number of people in that group are indoctrinated to believe things and behave in a certain restricted fashion, one can readily understand the staleness and lack of progress of such communities or groups.

"Doctrine is the necessary foundation of duty; if the theory is not correct, the practice cannot be right. Tell me what a man believes, and I will tell you what he will do." As two or more in a community begin to awaken to Self of their impersonal name (I AM), this True Identity of themselves will break the shackles of ignorance no matter how long a doctrine has enslaved the group or community. "Where two or more are gathered together in my name, "I" Am in the midst of them." (Matt. 18:20) *"I"* is True Identity of each of us.

All new birth of vegetation, minerals and animals, emerges from the invisible realm into visibility in Silence. The Source and Substance is infinite, never diminished in its capacity to supply needs to those who are sincere, open and receptive to Truth. Reliance on this Source for fulfillment, peace and joy is living by grace for "thy grace is my sufficiency in all things." (2 Cor. 9:8) In the throes of Self Reliance, one understands that the personal sense of self is as a shadow without substance and dies daily as the individual is tuned in to the inner station of I AM that broadcasts messages of inspiration, guidance, peace, protection or whatever the need may be. The mystery of this Source of givingness equates with the mystery of life that causes animals and plants to grow from within – in Silence. To observe the results of such growth from within encourages one to live wholly from within, to be Self-reliant in the eternal Now moment of peace, joy and fulfillment. Man, whose breath is in his nostrils – hu-man, who relies on his intellect – appears to be far removed from this secret peace place; yet it is always as close as his breathing. The momentum of habit, custom and tradition of the world enslaves him in ignorance.

Napoleon Hill, author of *Think and Grow Rich,* refers to two or more being on one accord as a Mastermind, where there is power in such a group far beyond the group itself. God created within man his own image and likeness, "I." As a mastermind group assembles, "I," the impersonal Self within, is in the midst of the group, the Mastermind. Whether it is an individual or a group endeavor, Silence is the gateway wherein "I" avails Itself into manifestation, earth. Beyond the horizon of the sense world lies spiritual discernment of my kingdom, spiritual substance of the universe. This is an all-spiritual universe manifesting as the world of the senses, form and experience. The "mastermind" principle must be used more often to realize solutions to problems of a community, society or nation. The personal sense of self, ego, is to be left out of the gathering of two or more, otherwise it will be an exercise in futility; the ego feeds off of bickering, arguments, disagreements, and other forms of dissension in always "wanting to be right." The mantra of ego says, "Be reasonable, do it my way."

Self Reliance is praying without ceasing (1 Thess. 5:17), for then the mind is empty of human thought and becomes an avenue of awareness for that still, small voice of Self. In silence of thoughts is the secret strength of a Mastermind being open to the flow of grace which brings forth new insight in solving any problems that confront the group. Individuals that comprise a mastermind group must practice being silent of thought in order to receive impartation from Self within. True prayer is not *talking* to God, but *listening*. The growing ability to experience Silence can be achieved by practicing the awareness exercise described earlier in this book.

"I" is with you always, even unto the end of the world. Trust It, rely on It, then you will know and understand Self Reliance. To awaken to Self, the Christ spirit within one's own being, is salvation and the realization of an uncovered peace that has always been with you. "Thy grace is my sufficiency in all things for my strength is made perfect in weakness" of humanhood. (2 Cor. 12:9)

To teach the young people Self Reliance at an early age will bring peace on earth, for their children will be birthed into a wholly new elevated consciousness that would approach being of the household of God. "If I be lifted up," that is, as consciousness rises to that of relying on the Inner Self of one's being, the indoctrination of the universal human belief of good and evil shall be shattered. Individually, however, one can repent of ignorance Now and truly be "born again" as one realizes that s/he, of the personal sense of self, is nothing.

In Self Reliance you must not outline in mind what you want the results to be. Living by the grace of God, one's True Self, is heaven on earth." In Self Reliance you are not required to think nor understand, simply be still, let and be a beholder of God's grace unfolding.

"When we can see beyond the appearance of evil, all of the Golden Grains of Good, we will love each other truly for then, we will be better understood."

BIOGRAPHY

Lewis Carter Baskins was born on a farm in Springfield, Arkansas. He attended racially segregated schools through grade school, high school and college. After graduating from AM&N College in Pine Bluff, Arkansas and two years in the U.S. Army he lived in Chicago, Ill., was accepted at and graduated from the University of Illinois College of Dentistry.

The interest in dentistry was sparked by a passing comment to him by a favorite high school teacher, "You have long fingers like a doctor."

Dr. Baskins is the father of four children, three sons and a daughter.

While yet practicing dentistry, his interest in the world of commercial business was intensified by a man who became his mentor, S.B. Fuller of Fuller Products Company. Baskins conducted sales meetings daily before opening his dental office. Many dental patients become salespeople of Fuller Products. Baskins wrote weekly articles for a community newspaper entitled, "As I See It."

Dr. Baskins's love of assisting people to grow in spiritual understanding led him to accept the invitation of a pastor to become an ordained minister for a number of years. He formulated the Institute of Attitude Modification (I AM) that hosted "Midweek Renewal Sessions" every Wednesday morning for a number of years and Sunday sessions called "A Celebration of Life" in the mornings and "Conversation for Transformation" on Sunday afternoon.

"Conversation for Transformation" continues to be hosted by Betty Muhammad and Dr. Baskins as of this writing, June 2015. Betty Muhammad and Dr. Baskins appear frequently on a local cable television station under the title "Success Made Easy."

Dr. Baskins has spoken at elementary and high schools as commencement speaker as well as during the regular school year for Career Day and as an inspirational speaker.

After retiring from dentistry as a dentist, Dr. Baskins continues to write and speak at schools and churches in Chicago, Ill. His passion is to share with those persons who are open and receptive, ideas that hundreds of people testify are beneficial in improving the quality of life experienced.

Dr. Baskins and Betty Muhammad have assisted individuals and groups in what is called "Anger Avoidance" in an effort to reduce conflict and/or violence among people by assisting them to awaken to their True Identity, thereby ceasing to pass judgment on others.

An internet television presentation can be accessed "on demand" at www.starplanettv.com entitled "Conversation for Transformation." Dr. Baskins and Betty Muhammad are the presenters. You can interact live with them on this website.

A "Return to Wellness" weekly national telephone conference call was instituted by Dr. Baskins and Betty Muhammad. These calls address wellness in the following areas: Physical Wellness, Financial Wellness, Relationship Wellness, Emotional Wellness and Spiritual Wellness. This endeavor was designed to offer insight into maintaining peace, harmony and joy in the life experience of the participants of the conference calls.

Made in the USA
Columbia, SC
26 January 2020